D1084633

SOCIETY FOR NEW TESTAMENT STUDIES

MONOGRAPH SERIES

General Editor: R. McL. Wilson, F.B.A.

Associate Editor: M. E. Thrall

49

'AND SO WE CAME TO ROME':
THE POLITICAL PERSPECTIVE
OF ST LUKE

'And so we came to Rome'

THE POLITICAL PERSPECTIVE OF ST LUKE

PAUL W. WALASKAY

Dean of Faculty and Professor of Biblical Literature,
Presbyterian School of Christian Education,
Richmond, Virginia

CAMBRIDGE UNIVERSITY PRESS

CAMBRIDGE
LONDON · NEW YORK · NEW ROCHELLE
MELBOURNE · SYDNEY

Published by the Press Syndicate of the University of Cambridge
The Pitt Building, Trumpington Street, Cambridge CB2 1RP
32 East 57th Street, New York, NY 10022, USA
296 Beaconsfield Parade, Middle Park, Melbourne 3206, Australia

First published 1983

Printed in Great Britain at the University Press, Cambridge

Library of Congress catalogue card number: 82–19835

British Library Cataloguing in Publication Data
Walaskay, Paul W.
'And so we came to Rome' : the political
perspective of St. Luke.–(Society
for New Testament Studies monographs
series; 49)
1. Bible. N.T. Luke–Commentaries
I. Title II. Series
226'. 406 BS2595.3
ISBN 0 521 25116 8

W. S.

TO MAXINE

Πολλαὶ θυγατέρες ἐκτήσαντο πλοῦτον,
πολλαὶ ἐποίησαν δυνατά,
σὺ δὲ ὑπέρκεισαι καὶ ὑπερῆρας πάσας.

Proverbs 31:29

CONTENTS

PREFACE

The observation that Luke—Acts contains a political component is, of course, not new. More than 250 years ago C. A. Heumann argued that Luke's two volumes were written 'as an apology for the Christian religion' to be presented to a Roman magistrate named Theophilus.[1] Through the 'storm center' and 'shifting sands' of recent Lucan research this aspect of Luke's writing has remained a strong rampart.[2] Though the analysis and interpretation of the political material in Luke—Acts has varied from scholar to scholar, the premise that Luke has presented an *apologia pro ecclesia* is constantly in the background. Those who are uneasy about the content, context, and objective of Luke's political apologetic conclude either that Luke has made an inconsistent *apologia pro ecclesia* or that apologetic concerns did not motivate him at all.[3]

Like others, I struggled with the problems raised by the Lucan *apologia* until it occurred to me that perhaps the premise was 'upside-down'; I had been reflecting on Acts 17:6 at the time. Could Luke rather have presented an *apologia pro imperio* to the early church? Reading Luke—Acts with this perspective in mind does clear away many of the problems consistently encountered in the traditional understanding of Luke's political apologetic.

In this book I shall review the development of the traditional perspective (Chapter 1), then raise three questions (Chapter 2): If Luke presents an *apologia pro ecclesia,* why does he include so much material that is politically damaging to the Christian cause? How does Luke handle the anti-Roman sentiment expressed in his sources? Are there passages in Luke—Acts that not only indicate a pro-Roman bias, but suggest an *apologia pro imperio*? I answer the last question in the affirmative, a conclusion supported by an investigation of the text of Luke—Acts, particularly the trials of Jesus (Chapter 3) and Paul (Chapter 4).

Luke's pro-Roman perspective suggested to his readers that the institutions of church and empire are coeval and complementary. According to this perspective, the Christian church and the Roman empire need not fear nor suspect each other, for God stands behind both institutions giving to each the power and the authority to carry out his will. That the Christian church survived that first crucial century may be due in large measure to the cautious wisdom of Luke in this regard (Chapter 5).

I wish to express my gratitude to my friends and colleagues at Colgate Rochester Divinity School, Duke University, and the University of Rochester who assisted, supported, and encouraged me in this work. I am deeply indebted to Professor Franklin W. Young of Duke University, whose sage counsel and criticism have been as valuable to me as his personal warmth and understanding.

I am particularly grateful to Professor R. McLachlan Wilson and Professor Margaret E. Thrall who carefully guided this book through its final, but most critical stage. Whatever strengths one finds in this work reflect the wisdom of my mentors and editors; its weaknesses are my own.

My thanks also to President Robert Sproull, Provost Richard O'Brien, and Dr Clifford Reifler of the University of Rochester who granted me the time necessary to write my final draft, and to Mrs Rebecca Hurysz, my secretary, who calmly prepared that draft in spite of my mounting anxiety and deteriorating scrawl.

Finally, without the distracting playfulness of my daughter Rachel this work might have progressed faster, but it would have been far less enjoyable; and without the affection and encouragement of my wife Maxine the work might never have been done at all.

Paul W. Walaskay

ABBREVIATIONS

AB   Anchor Bible Commentary

ASNU   Acta Seminarii Neotestamentici Upsaliensis

BC   *The Beginnings of Christianity*, 5 vols., ed. by F. J. Foakes Jackson and K. Lake, London, 1920–33

BD   *A Greek Grammar of the New Testament and Other Early Christian Literature*, F. Blass and A. DeBrunner, Chicago, 1961

BZ   *Biblische Zeitschrift*

CAH   *Cambridge Ancient History*, 12 vols., ed. by S. A. Cook, E. E. Adcock and M. P. Charlesworth, Cambridge, 1923–39

CBC   Cambridge Bible Commentary

CBQ   *Catholic Biblical Quarterly*

CQR   *Church Quarterly Review*

FIRA   *Fontes iuris romani antejustiniani*, 3 vols., ed. by S. Riccobono, Florence, 1940–43

HTR   *Harvard Theological Review*

HThKNT   Herder's Theologischer Kommentar zum Neuen Testament

HNT   Handbuch zum Neuen Testament

HNTC   Harper's New Testament Commentary

ICC   International Critical Commentary

JBL   *Journal of Biblical Literature*

JAOS   *Journal of the American Oriental Society*

JRS   *Journal of Roman Studies*

JTS   *Journal of Theological Studies*

KEK   Kritisch-exegetischer Kommentar über das Neue Testament

LCL   Loeb Classical Library

MLA   *The Making of Luke–Acts*, H. J. Cadbury, London, 1927

MNTC   Moffatt New Testament Commentary

NCB   New Century Bible

NovT   *Novum Testamentum*

NTS   *New Testament Studies*

PCB   *Peake's Commentary on the Bible*, ed. by M Black and H. H. Rowley, London, 1962

1

INTRODUCTION

Luke wanted to help his reader comprehend not only the events of the early church, but also the *meaning* of those events in the context of Hellenistic culture.[1] When he moves from the world of *data* to the world of *meaning*, the reader is invited to contemplate the relationship of God to the world. Luke is not only a historian, but a theologian as well.[2]

When the shift is made from 'Luke the historian' to 'Luke the theologian' the scope of Luke's contributions is greatly broadened; not only descriptive history, but apology and eschatology as well fall under the control of Luke's theology.[3] Furthermore, all these interdependent elements form a complex, but unified, theology. For example, eschatology must be continually thought through in relation to ongoing history, and occasionally the circumstances of history force some of that thinking to take on apologetic qualities. And apology not only deals with present circumstance by recalling history, but should assist the faithful as they look with hope toward the future, the *eschaton*.

History, apology, and eschatology form interrelated components of Luke's theology. If *history* describes where the community *has been* and *eschatology* describes where it is *going*, then *apology* describes where the community *is now*. Apology locates the community in the inescapable realities of the present situation, and apology speaks to the community about its status in this situation, drawing on events of the past and visions of the future. It is Luke's apology, his theology of the present, which we shall investigate in this work.

Most commentators, from the nineteenth-century tendency critics to the current redaction critics, consider the Lucan apology to be outer-directed, an *apologia pro ecclesia* presented to Rome. This may be true; but if so, it is only part of Luke's apologetic motive. Above all, like all other New Testament authors, Luke has written to his own community and has laid before them items with which they should be concerned. Therefore, when we suggest that Luke addressed the Christian community, then his political apology may also, or even primarily, be an *apologia pro imperio*.

1

Before diverging from the traditional viewpoint regarding Luke's apologetic, it would be a useful and stimulating exercise to walk again along the narrow path first beaten by the Tübingen school, then followed, with few venturings off into the woods, by a century of scholars.

A. The Tübingen approach

The figure that towers over almost every aspect of New Testament scholarship is Ferdinand Christian Baur. Nowhere does his figure cast a larger shadow than on the apologetic found in Acts. Developing a thesis first laid down by J. Griesbach and H. E. G. Paulus, Baur claimed that Acts was an irenic and apologetic work written by a Paulinist (not Luke) to defend Paul's mission to the gentiles.[4] The Jewish Christian wing of the church with its particularistic, legalistic point of view was engaged in confrontation with the universalistic, 'libertine' Paulinist Christians. Acts, the work of a great synthesizer, is the 'Hegelian product' of a first-century thesis (Jewish Christianity) and antithesis (Pauline Christianity). Acts was written as a document of peace which would facilitate the reunification of two warring factions. As a result, Peter is pictured as less of a legalist than the Jewish Christians remembered him and Paul as more yielding toward the Jerusalem council than his letter to the Galatians indicates. The author of Acts has retouched the historical apostolic portrait to fit the needs of his own divided church. At the same time he attempted to defend Paul and restore him to a place of honor within the whole Christian community. By showing that the apostle's background and teaching lay within the boundaries of Judaism, the author of Acts has implied that Paul and his churches need not be excluded from the wider community of faith.

While Baur was developing the view that the author of Acts presented an internal apologetic intended to reconcile church factions, Karl Schrader and Matthias Schneckenburger were calling attention to another dimension of the apology. Acts was also intended to quell the anxieties of the church as it began to settle into the secular world. It was this urbane, political world of the Roman empire, far removed from the provincial life of Palestine, which challenged the new sect's expansive policy toward non-Jews. This policy raised questions for Roman officialdom as to the legitimate place of Christianity within the household of Judaism, an especially critical issue for Jewish Christians.

According to Schrader the surprising ending of Acts suggests that the book was intended to maximize the impression that Christianity was an innocent religion. Therefore the author leaves off not with the death of

Paul at the hands of Nero (a story which the author knows but suppresses), but with the free and unhindered preaching of the apostle in Rome.[5]

Schneckenburger saw that aside from defending Paul's personal and apostolic behavior to the Jewish Christians, Luke has also defended the political legitimacy of Paul. Paul's position with regard to the gentiles will not, according to the Lucan apologetic, endanger the legal status of the Jewish Christians in Rome. The many acquittals of Paul by Roman authorities prove this.[6]

Finally, Edward Zeller, in his comprehensive presentation of the Tübingen theory of ecclesiastical development, commended Schneckenburger for having proved beyond all doubt that the apologetic motif in Luke's second volume was to reconcile Jewish Christians and Paulinists at the expense of extreme claims made by both.[7] Like Schneckenburger, Zeller found two strands of apologetics in Acts and, like Baur, he saw that apologetic and irenic material stand side by side. The object of the composition of Acts, Zeller concluded, was first to defend the work of Paul among the gentiles by tempering the word and work of Paul and the Jewish Christians, thus reconciling the Jewish Christians and Paulinists of Luke's own day; Acts was a mediating work intended for both parties. Secondly, Acts was an attempt to conciliate the Roman government and to prove the harmlessness of Christianity. Paul, after all, was acquitted before the Roman authorities.[8]

B. The reaction against Tübingen

Perhaps the only verity in the uncertain world of the academy is that action invites reaction. It was not long before New Testament scholars mounted a devastating attack against the Tübingen conciliatory hypothesis.[9] A. J. Mattill has concisely spelled out the major fronts of this attack:

> (1) Since Jewish Christianity lost its power after AD 70, it could not have played the role in the second century ascribed to it by the Tübingen theory. (2) Peter and Paul were in basic agreement, not two hostile Apostles heading two hostile parties preaching two hostile gospels in two hostile missions. (3) Early church history cannot be fitted into the Hegelian categories of thesis (Petrine Christianity), antithesis (Pauline Christianity), and synthesis (Old Catholic Church). (4) Nor did Luke deliberately falsify positively his narrative in the interests of a tendency.[10]

Although the conciliatory tendency of Luke's writing was called into serious question, the *apologia pro ecclesia* did not undergo the same scrutiny; if anything, it was raised to greater importance in the discussion of Luke's purpose. Kümmel puts the issue clearly: 'If in Acts there appears *no inner Christian apologetic*, we still cannot fail to recognize *the purpose of defending the Christians* against the charge of hostility toward the state.'[11]

Johannes Weiss, in his classic study *Über die Absicht und den literarischen Charakter der Apostel-Geschichte*, asserted that the controlling purpose of Acts was to set Christianity right with the Roman government. Moreover Luke's apologetic was not limited to his second volume, but appeared in his gospel as well.[12] Weiss, taking his cue from Zeller, saw in the Lucan apologetic more than a mere defense of Paul before Caesar; the church itself was on trial. The two charges laid against Christians by the Jewish community were: (1) Christians were apostates from Judaism and (2) the new religion was dangerous to the state and ought not to be recognized as a *religio licita*.[13] According to Weiss, Luke's response was: (1) Christianity was born in Judaism but supplanted it in the Roman world. It was Christianity that took the world-wide vision of the Old Testament prophets seriously and developed that vision into a universal mission. Christianity, therefore, is the true Judaism which deserves imperial protection. (2) Christians are also loyal citizens; Paul was continually acquitted by Roman magistrates. Therefore, even as Paul was tolerated by the Roman government, so should the new religion be tolerated as a *religio licita*.[14]

At the same time that Weiss was promoting his view of the Lucan purpose in Germany, Professor William Ramsay was lecturing on a similar theme in Great Britain and America. The substance of these important lectures was published under the title *St. Paul the Traveller and the Roman Citizen*. Ramsay concluded this work with a discussion of Luke's legal defense of Paul. If Christianity was to survive as a legally constituted religion, then it needed a test case which would insure its continuance; the trial of Paul provided for Luke just such a case. Ramsay speculated that Paul was eventually acquitted in Rome and

> if he was acquitted, the issue of the trial was a formal decision by the supreme court of the empire that it was permissible to preach Christianity; the trial, therefore, was really a charter of religious liberty and therein lies its immense importance. It was, indeed, overturned by later decisions of the supreme court; but its existence was a highly important fact for the Christians.[15]

C. A classical presentation of Luke's *apologia pro ecclesia*

With the notable exception of Harald Sahlin who attempted to revive the
notion that Acts was actually written as a trial brief for Paul,[16] the weight
of twentieth-century critical scholarship has been on the side of Weiss and
Ramsay who saw that the Pauline defense was a veneer; the substance of
Luke's writing was a defense of the church. The disciples of Weiss and
Ramsay are legion. Because it would be a lengthy and redundant exercise
to review the position of each scholar, we shall limit ourselves to one of
the more comprehensive studies of Luke's apologetic.[17]

In 1927 Henry J. Cadbury published his classic study, *The Making of
Luke–Acts*. In his chapter on 'The Object of Luke–Acts' Cadbury attempts to link the apologetic purpose of Acts with the Third Gospel. To
begin, Cadbury typically suggests that no one motive is necessarily the
dominant force behind the writing of Luke–Acts; one finds a variety
of motives embedded in the text.[18]

One feature that pervades the entire two volumes, however, is a divinely
ordered sequence of historical events which occur through Jesus, the
disciples, and the church – what we have come to call *Heilsgeschichte*.
A corollary to the proposition that God is working in the world through
his servants is the notion that this divine activity is the fulfillment of
Old Testament prophecy.[19] It is for this reason that Christianity stands
squarely within the camp of Judaism.

A second theme running through Luke–Acts is a concern to proclaim
the political loyalty of the church. Luke was compelled to raise a defense
against the charges that Christianity may act or even exist in violation of
Roman law.

> It may even be conjectured that his Jewish apologetic had as its
> aim the satisfaction of Rome's demand that foreign religions
> must be licensed to be permitted. If Judaism was a *religio licita*
> and Christianity was not, it was important to show that Christian-
> ity was only a legitimate form of Judaism and could shelter under
> the Jewish name.[20]

Even if this argument succeeded, there still remained the scandal of
Jesus' cross and Paul's chains. Some explanation was necessary if the
Christian community was to be seen as innocent in the sight of Rome.
Therefore it would be natural for Luke

> to attempt to avert the superficial impression which the experi-
> ences of Jesus and Paul might make. Even the repeated statements
> that the Romans exonerated them were not enough. It must be

explained why when innocent they were arrested, why when
acquitted they were not yet freed.[21]

Cadbury suggests three possible explanations.

First, it may be conjectured that 'the Jews took the initiative ... due in
part to the Christians' own hostility to the Jews, possibly in part to a
desire to "whitewash" the Romans.'[22] The Book of Acts is replete with
'plots of the Jews' against the Christian movement. Cadbury concludes
tongue-in-cheek that 'Paul would be almost pleasantly surprised to hear
the leading Jews in Rome say, "We neither received letters from Judea
concerning thee, nor did any of the brethren come hither and report or
speak any harm of thee ... "'[23]

Secondly, the Roman magistrates may have realized that they were
involved in internal Jewish controversies which 'were not justiciable,
or were so obscure that procurators and proconsuls could not fathom
them.'[24] These Jews, after all, were simply arguing over words, names,
and fine points of Jewish law, matters beyond the competency of the
Roman judiciary. Even though Paul was arrested as a disturber of the
peace 'the trouble was never an overt act of Paul, but either the malevol-
ence of the Jews, selfish financial considerations or mere misunderstanding,
and so Paul suffered, though innocent.'[25]

Finally, Cadbury points out that in Luke's presentation the Romans
acted kindly toward Paul.

> The proconsul in Cyprus and the *Primus* in Malta welcomed
> him, the Asiarchs in Ephesus became his friends and sheltered
> him, Roman soldiers repeatedly defended him from violence,
> treated him with kindness and respect, and stood in awe of his
> Roman citizenship when they discovered it.[26]

This type of treatment would hardly be expected by one seriously suspected of *lèse majesté*.

While one cannot be certain that Luke has written a brief for Paul's
trial, Cadbury concludes that

> several of the words in the address to Theophilus do permit, and
> when compared with the latter part of Acts positively possess,
> the connotation of *apologia*, and that the close of Acts itself
> is filled with that mood. It is quite probable that Luke's avowed
> purpose so far as his preface expresses it, 'that thou mightest
> know the certainty concerning the things wherein thou wast
> instructed,' is to correct misinformation about Christianity ...[27]

And so the Lucan apologetic purpose which is not at all obvious at the beginning of the Third Gospel is made crystal clear as the reader reaches the last section of Acts. Luke, having dramatically built up this two-volume *apologia pro ecclesia*, returned to the beginning of his work and, with the apologetic purpose in mind, penned his preface to Theophilus.[28]

H. J. Cadbury's work has, for the past half-century, established the high-water mark in Lucan studies. Drawing together Greek, Roman, and Oriental influences, literary, social, and political backgrounds, Cadbury has applied this body of knowledge to the text of Luke–Acts with un-surpassed insight. He concluded that Luke was primarily a historian following the historiographic conventions of his time;[29] throughout this history of Jesus and the church there are traces of Luke's intention to defend the innocence of his religion.

D. The redaction critical school

Following World War II, the weight of critical scholarship shifted back again to Germany where scholars were busily teasing out the theological themes imbedded in Luke–Acts. R. Bultmann began to probe behind the presentation of 'Luke the historian' by asking a basic question: 'Why did Luke write at all?' This, of course, may be asked of any of the gospel writers. But Luke wrote more than a gospel; he added a second volume on the history of the church – why? Bultmann suggested that Luke had lost the original eschatological understanding of Jesus, presenting in its place a history of Jesus and the church.[30] As every student of the New Testament knows, the scholarly storm broke with Hans Conzelmann who, using the redaction critical method, found Bultmann's suggestion con-firmed in Luke's theology.

Contemporary New Testament scholars are deeply indebted to Hans Conzelmann and his exciting research on the Third Gospel and Acts. His *Die Mitte der Zeit* represents the first serious and comprehensive appli-cation of redaction criticism to the writings of Luke.[31] For three decades, form critics had atomized the synoptic gospels into their component parts, analyzed each part thoroughly, and then deposited the parts into appropriate categories. By 1950 the redaction critical school was ready to look once again at the gospels as wholes. Bits and fragments of a gospel could not be left in compartments labelled 'Sermons,' 'Paradigms,' 'Tales,' and so on. The evangelists were not merely collectors, assemblers, and transmitters of pieces of traditional material, but authors and theologians. Each gospel writer had a story to tell; the message he spoke to his church was his own message. Though the material the evangelist used may be from written or oral sources, the very *way* in which he used it, the words and phrases he included or omitted, the order in which he put the pieces of tradition, and his turning from the sources to set down his own thoughts point to the particular perspective of the evangelist.

Conzelmann has opened our eyes to a wide variety of motifs found in the Third Gospel and Acts: Luke's unusual presentation of Palestinian geography, his dealing with the problems raised by a delayed parousia, and the Lucan presentation of the threefold epochs in salvation history. The motif which is of most interest to us is a corollary of Luke's resolution to the problems raised by the delayed parousia. Conzelmann states the situation well:

> As life in the world continues, there arise certain problems
> concerning the relation of the church to its environment, which
> had remained hidden at the beginning because of the belief that
> the end was imminent. It is a question mainly of the relation-
> ship of the church with Judaism and with the empire, and it is
> significant how Luke deals with these problems. He engages in
> apologetic.[32]

Like his Tübingen predecessors, Conzelmann suggests that the Lucan apologetic was double-pronged to be used both *internally* and *externally*.[33] But unlike his predecessors who felt that the *internal apologetic* was intended to reconcile disparate wings of *Christianity*, Conzelmann con- cludes that the *internal apologetic* was designed to settle the religious disputes between sects of *'Israel.'* The Christian sect of Judaism 'must obey God rather than men,' an argument which, according to Conzelmann, is never used with regard to the civil government. At the same time Luke's apologetic was used *externally as a defense of the church before the state.*

Though Conzelmann may be correct in his view that Luke represented early Christianity as one sect of Judaism which needed an internal apolo- getic directed to the wider Jewish community, it is the external defense, the defense of the church before the state, which is more problematic. Here Conzelmann follows in the footsteps of Zeller, Weiss, Ramsay, and Cadbury by stating that the political apologetic of Luke is directed to the state on behalf of the church; Christians are loyal and apolitical subjects. Like Cadbury and Weiss, Conzelmann sees elements of this apologetic in the gospel as well as in Acts:

Luke 3:19.	A nonpolitical reason is given for John's arrest.
4:16–19.	Jesus' sermon reveals a nonpolitical program.
13:31–5.	Jesus is to die as a prophet not as a political messiah.

19:38.   In the presentation of Jesus' entry into Jerusalem, Luke has replaced 'the concept of Davidic lordship ... by the simple title of King, the nonpolitical sense of which is preserved.'[34]

20:20–6.   Jesus (and Luke) uphold the political supremacy of Rome.

21:12–15.   Jesus encourages his diciples to bear witness even to kings and governors for ' ... to confess oneself to be a Christian implies no crime against Roman law.'[35]

23:1–5.   The accusation of the Jews against Jesus was a lie (as it still is against the church), and there would be no Roman intervention at all if it were not for Jewish agitation.

23:22.   The Roman procurator has for a third time found Jesus to be politically innocent.

All of this, according to Conzelmann, represents an implied political apologetic in the Third Gospel. There is also evidence of political apologetic in the Acts of the Apostles:

10:1ff.   The first pagan convert to Christianity is a low-ranking official of the Roman government.

13:6–12.   A somewhat higher Roman official is astonished not only by the miraculous conduct of Paul, but also by the 'teaching of the Lord.'

16:35–9.   Luke makes the first mention of Paul's Roman citizenship.

17:6–7.   Luke makes it 'quite clear what the political problem is';[36] Paul and Silas have 'turned the world upside-down' and now the whole Christian community is 'acting against the decrees of Caesar, saying that there is another king, Jesus.'

In Acts, however, Luke has gone further than an implied defense of the church by presenting an explicit political apologetic.

In the last quarter of Acts the terms $\dot{\alpha}\pi o\lambda o\gamma\epsilon\tilde{\iota}\sigma\theta\alpha\iota$ and $\dot{\alpha}\pi o\lambda o\gamma\acute{\iota}\alpha$ are purposely used in determining the legal position of Christianity within the empire. The problem which places Luke on the greatest defensive is not the relationship between Judaism and Christianity (this belongs to the internal category of apologetic), but the relationship between Christianity and the state.

Conzelmann has wisely observed that the Lucan political apologetic is not an appeal for religious toleration under the protective law of *religio licita*, but an appeal to the state to extend civil rights equitably and fairly to all its citizens including Christian citizens.[37] Paul is not protected by his Judaism but by his citizenship. Luke argues that when it becomes necessary, the Christian should be allowed his 'day in court,' including his right of appeal to the emperor.

Conzelmann's work is provocative and exciting; it has stimulated two decades of discussion about Luke's theology. Yet, none of the major redaction critics has dealt seriously with his assumptions about the Lucan apologetic.[38] Much of Conzelmann's discussion about the political apologetic in Luke–Acts is unclear and, at times, contradictory.

Some of this haziness is perhaps due to Conzelmann's indecision about whether or not Luke consciously attempted to deal with the political situation of his own church. In the *Festschrift* for Paul Schubert, *Studies in Luke–Acts*, Conzelmann states that Luke pursues *no political interests*.[39] Yet in his *Theology of St. Luke* he states that 'Luke's apologetic aims are political.'[40] What is Conzelmann's assumption about Luke's message? Can Luke present Christianity as an apolitical movement while making a political defense for the faith? Conzelmann's inconsistency reveals his own uneasiness about the Lucan apologetic.

Furthermore Conzelmann's rather sketchy foray into some of the 'political' passages in the Third Gospel and Acts raises serious questions which Conzelmann avoids, ignores, or overlooks. For example, is Jesus' program as apolitical as Conzelmann suggests, especially when one considers the potential political impact of Jesus' Old Testament text and the sermon which he preached to a Galilean synagogue? And when Luke changes the cry of the crowd from Mark's 'Blessed is *the one* who comes in the name of the Lord' to 'Blessed is *the king* who comes in the name of the Lord,' can we really consider Luke's addition to be an apolitical statement about Jesus? Also we must ask why it is that Luke's emphasis on imperial innocence at the trial of Jesus would be important to an imperial official? Is Luke really addressing this external apologetic to the Romans or is it meant for internal use in the Christian community?

Finally, though Conzelmann is correct in stressing that in Acts there is no attempt to prove that Christianity is a *religio licita*,[41] he does the Lucan Paul a disservice and misunderstands Luke the Paulinist by claiming that 'in connection with the State *only* political and legal arguments are used.'[42] As we shall see in the discussion of Paul's trial, that simply is not true; Luke does not so neatly divorce 'religious apologetic' from 'political apologetic'. Rather, political and religious issues are always interwoven in Paul's legal defense.

E. The current perspective

An unbroken chain of scholars has insisted that one of Luke's primary purposes was to present an *apologia pro ecclesia*. Zeller, Weiss, Ramsay, Cadbury, Conzelmann – all have carefully worked through the Lucan literature and all have come to virtually the same conclusion about Luke's apology. This perspective continues, though not without serious misgivings; the uneasiness about this pillar of faith seems to be growing. Recent scholars have been poking here and there at the evidence, raising tentative doubts about the traditional view of Luke's apology, yet unable to put a finger on the core of the problem.

Robert Karris, for example, recognizes that there is a serious problem in describing the first-century church as a victim of Roman persecution; it is impossible to find evidence of clear-cut persecution of Christianity by the Roman government.[43] At most one might say 'that the Jews may have been behind the Roman persecution of Christians.'[44] Karris' conclusion is inconclusive: ' ... more in-depth work needs to be done on the persecution, harassment, and distress situation in Luke–Acts ... '[45]

Karris is quite right when he notes that Luke's 'persecuted [!] Christian reader ... might have strained to see the consistency of the answers which Luke ... gave to the problems of faith which persecution had stirred up in his being.'[46] Yes, Luke is an inconsistent apologist for the early church, as the next chapter makes clear. Therefore we must ask if the inconsistency may, in fact, be due to *our* perceptions of the situation of the first-century church and not due to any muddle-headedness on the part of Luke.

Luke's church probably was not, as Conzelmann has termed it, an *ecclesia pressa*. Jesus was indeed crucified, Stephen was martyred, and Paul was both persecutor and persecuted, but according to Luke these were unfortunate, though necessary, parts of God's design for salvation;[47] perhaps an extension of J. M. Creed's statement – there is 'no *theologia crucis*' in Luke–Acts – is in order.[48] Such events call for no Christian political defense, especially not to a Roman magistrate. They are part of the ebb and flow of God's design for salvation which cannot be thwarted by Roman court, Jewish Sanhedrin, nor mob violence.

As a result of this uneasiness about Luke's 'inconsistencies,' scholars are content to conclude that Luke's political apologetic motive is either secondary or non-existent. E. Franklin arrives at the former conclusion. Luke has rewritten the trial of Jesus to shift the blame for Jesus' death from the Romans to the Jews. Yet, no matter how hard Luke may try to cover over the facts of the case, the final responsibility for Jesus'

condemnation lay in Roman hands.[49] Likewise, Paul's trial abounds
with judicial inconsistencies which would again raise questions about the
fairness of Roman procedure and the soundness of Paul's case. Furthermore, if the outcome of Paul's trial was favorable, Luke, by not mentioning the verdict, has thrown away a golden opportunity to vindicate
the Christian cause.[50] Franklin concludes that Luke is less interested in
defending Christians or Romans than he is in 'presenting additional
material regarding Jewish perversity.'[51]

But we must ask *why* Luke took such pains in casting the Jews in an
unfavorable light and *why* Roman deficiencies were so often glossed over.
Even though Luke's primary purpose may not have been to offer an
apology to Rome on behalf of the church, he certainly seems to be saying
something of importance about the value of convivial Roman–Christian
relationships. Thus, Gerhard Schneider and Walter Radl suggest that
Luke's purpose, while not apologetic in any rigid sense, was to steer his
community along a precarious path which cuts through the tempting
fields of overly accommodating conformity and non-compromising confrontation with the state.[52] At the end of the path lies the possibility not
of mere survival in the empire, but of dialogue between Christians and
Romans. I would add that Luke attempted to initiate this dialogue by
putting Rome's 'best foot forward'; his apology is *pro imperio*.

Finally, Richard Cassidy, in a recent study, has concluded that Luke
was not attempting a political apologetic at all. He attacks Conzelmann's
view that Luke presented an *apologia pro ecclesia* on two fronts: first,
Conzelmann has failed to deal with those passages 'in which Luke shows
Jesus refusing to cooperate with, or actually criticizing, his political
rulers'; secondly, Conzelmann has not sufficiently appreciated 'Luke's
portrayal of Jesus as one who consistently contravened the existing
social patterns ... which the Romans were committed to maintain.'[53]

Having pointed out these major weaknesses Cassidy offers his own threefold argument which leads him to conclude that Luke had no apologetic
motive in mind as he set pen to parchment. First, in the Third Gospel
Jesus frequently contravenes the existing social patterns and does not
defer to political authority. Throughout his book Cassidy cites three
pieces of evidence to support this: Luke 13:31–3 (Jesus refers to Herod
as 'that fox'), 22:24–7 (Jesus criticizes the kings of the gentiles for
'dominating' their subjects), and 21:12–15 (Jesus' warning that the
disciples will be brought before kings and governors). Unfortunately,
these citations raise more questions about Luke's political stance than
they solve. Jesus hears at second hand that Herod wants to kill him;
when later 'that fox' has the opportunity (Luke 23:6–16), he lets it

slip by.[54] If Luke was presenting a negative picture of Herodian (not necessarily Roman) authority, why did he so obviously downplay one of the best attested stories about the vile tetrarch, the beheading of John the Baptist?[55] A thorough exegesis of Jesus' 'critique' of the gentile kings renders not a negative, but a positive evaluation of their authority.[56] And Luke may simply be repeating his source's prediction that the disciples will bear witness to kings and governors; this is not, for Luke, an evil, but an opportunity.

Cassidy's second argument against the notion that Luke wrote with an apologetic motive relies on his investigation of Jesus' trial. While I agree with many of Cassidy's observations about the trial (Pilate too quickly and facilely pronounced Jesus innocent of a serious charge; Luke has subtly eased the blame for Jesus' death from the Romans to the Jews), I would disagree that this reveals *no* political apologetic concern. At very least Luke has shaded the historical evidence to favor the Romans, an implicit *apologia pro imperio*.

Finally, Cassidy makes the point that Luke chose not to conceal Jesus' Zealot contacts. This certainly argues against the traditional view concerning Luke's apology. A Roman official could not but have wondered about such friends of Jesus.

While Cassidy has raised some notions about Jesus' social program that provoke one's thinking about the gospel as it challenges our own society, he has not always rigorously followed through with his redaction critical analysis. One is left with a tendentious, but rather flat, reconstruction of Luke's political perspective. Though Jesus may have confronted the 'powers that be' in Palestine, one is not so sure that Luke was as willing to extend that challenge to Rome.

Cassidy, Karris, and the others do point to the nagging difficulty with respect to recovering Luke's political perspective. Scholars are forced to twist the data to fit Luke's *apologia pro ecclesia*,[57] to suggest that Luke was not so concerned with an apologetic after all, or to throw in the towel and admit that Luke simply had no apologetic intentions. Given the great amount of material in Luke−Acts devoted to the politics of the early empire I am not eager to dismiss the possibility that Luke was politically motivated. And given the peculiar and 'inconsistent' political perspective of Luke I would be reluctant to claim that he writes to some Roman magistrate. There is, however, another option open to us: that Luke was decidedly pro-Roman and he intended, in part, to present an apologetic on behalf of the empire to his own church.

Conzelmann is correct at least on one point: the church, Luke has wisely ascertained, is going to continue its earthly existence within the political context of the Roman empire. One can damn the social circumstances to an apocalyptic hell and withdraw, or one can, as best as one's conscience may allow, try to come to terms with the political, cultural, and social context for the sake of further expansion. One should at least point out those positive items that are worthy of mention; and one should recall that God stands behind *all* human institutions as the power who delegates all authority.

2

THE POLITICS OF LUKE: A REAPPRAISAL

For the past quarter-millenium biblical scholars have generally supported C. A. Heumann's suggestion that Luke's purpose was to write an *apologia pro ecclesia* to a Roman magistrate named Theophilus.[1] This point of view has consistently encountered serious exegetical difficulties. Perhaps the way out of these difficulties is to reverse Heumann's proposal. Luke, intending his narrative *for the church*, has skewed the political nuances of his sources toward a *pro-Roman perspective*. But before proclaiming too loudly this solution to the problem of Luke's political apologetic, we must examine three items.

First, we need to re-examine the hypothesis that a Roman official reading Luke–Acts would have concluded that Christianity was politically harmless. Secondly, if we are to see Luke's work as pro-Roman, then the 'anti-Roman' material in Luke–Acts must be considered. Finally, we must examine the way Luke has reworked his sources in order to attain a pro-Roman perspective. This leads to a detailed investigation of the political apologetic in the lengthy trial narratives of the Third Gospel (Chapter 3) and Acts (Chapter 4).

A. Did Luke present a politically harmless picture of Christianity?

Most commentators who discuss Luke's political apologetic are quite one-sided in selecting material from Luke–Acts.[2] It is certainly true that Luke wrote much that might have impressed a Roman authority with the political harmlessness of the church: Jesus was declared innocent by Pontius Pilate, Paul was treated fairly and justly by Roman magistrates, and the attitude of the Roman government toward the church was generally neutral. The highlighting of such passages in Luke–Acts, however, obscures several scenes that would certainly have raised questions about the political innocence of the church.

15

1. Simon, the so-called Zealot (Luke 6: 15; Acts 1: 13)

In Luke 6: 15 the Third Evangelist boldly declares what his source (Mark 3: 18) attempted to conceal: that Jesus had among his disciples at least one Zealot.[3] In the five other instances where Mark transliterated an Aramaic term, he gave an appropriate Greek equivalent. Thus, James and John are surnamed 'Boanerges, *that is*, sons of thunder'.[4] Had Mark been consistent, and less afraid to make the meaning clear to his readers, he would have made the addendum: 'Simon the Cananaean, which means, the Zealot.'

Two suggestions have been advanced to explain why Luke made certain that his readers knew that Simon was a Zealot. First, Luke was sufficiently removed from the Jewish war, both spatially and temporally, for the odium felt for the Jewish rebels to have dissipated.[5] Yet, if Luke wrote approximately ten years after the fall of Jerusalem, that is not an especially long time to have forgotten this particularly bitter war. The stigma of the term 'Zealot' would have remained with the returning troops.

Secondly, Luke really intended 'Zealot' to be taken in a strictly pious sense.[6] But Luke did not specify, as he did for others, that Simon was 'zealous for the law' or 'zealous towards God.' [7] Furthermore, we must ask if it was because of habit, coincidence, or colloquialism that in mentioning Simon, Luke used a phrase similar to Josephus' statements about the rebels. In Luke, Simon is τὸν καλούμενον Ζηλωτήν; in Josephus, the rebels are τῶν κληθέντων Ζηλωτῶν.[8]

It is unlikely that Luke 6: 15 was ever intended for the ears of a Roman official. Rather the passage provided Luke a means of speaking clearly to the Christian community about the extent of Jesus' involvement with the Zealots. The disciples, including Simon the Zealot, have heard and accepted Jesus' saying that the authority to fix the events of history, which included the restoration of the kingdom to Israel, rests not with them but with God. At the beginning of Acts, the risen Lord proclaims that they shall indeed be given power (δύναμις) not for revolution but for witnessing.[9] What was once a burning desire to overthrow the imperial presence in Judea must, in the face of the need to spread the gospel, die with Jesus and be resurrected to a new concept of missionary zealotry.

2. Jesus' command to buy swords (Luke 22: 35–8)

In Luke 22: 35–8 Jesus reverses his requirements at the first commissioning of the disciples. Whereas once Jesus sent his disciples 'with no purse nor bag nor sandals' to preach the gospel in the countryside, now in the last days of his life Jesus commands them to take their purse and bag, and 'let him who has no sword sell his mantle and buy one' (Luke 9:1– 3). The disciples proudly proclaim their preparedness in response to Jesus.

No matter whether one today understands this command literally or interprets it metaphorically,[10] a first-century Roman official, especially one not well disposed toward Christianity, would have been disturbed by Jesus' statement. If Luke was trying to impress such an official, he might have conveniently omitted this command,[11] for this could only have been a stumbling-block for a Roman official. Nevertheless, a Christian, by reading further, would seriously contemplate the conclusion to the sword episode. While Jesus had allowed the disciples to make their own calculations for defense, he also established a limit of active resistance. In the garden, at the moment of confrontation with the Jewish authorities, Jesus set the limit: 'You may go thus far, but no farther' (Luke 22:51). The disciples had confronted the Jewish pawns of Rome, but here political conflict must cease. By implication, Rome itself must not be confronted.

3. Jesus as lord and king (Luke 19:38 and Acts 1:6)

It has been noted that the 'most characteristic title of Jesus in Luke– Acts is ὁ κύριος.'[12] Franklin points out that Luke not only used κύριε as a title of respect, but also in its fullest sense of kingly sovereignty. The disciples greeted the resurrected Christ: 'Lord, will you at this time restore sovereignty (βασιλείαν) to Israel?' (Acts 1:6). Jesus neither denied his lordship, nor dampened the hope of his disciples for a national kingdom. Nor did Luke attempt to construct a non-political gloss on the church's claim that Jesus is Lord and Christ.

In Mark 11:9 the crowd acclaimed Jesus as '*he* who comes in the name of the Lord.' Luke changed the triumphal greeting to, 'Blessed is the *king* who comes in the name of the Lord.' While it is certainly true that Luke has replaced the ambiguous concept of Davidic kingship 'by the simple title of king,'[13] this hardly renders the Lucan text, as Conzelmann suggests, non-political. Luke could not more clearly have raised a question about Christian loyalties in the mind of a Roman reader.

From the beginning of his Gospel to its close, Luke unambiguously presented Jesus as a king.

> He will be great, and will be called
>   the Son of the Most High
>   and the Lord God will give to him
>   the throne of his father David,

> and he will reign (βασιλεύσει) over the house of
> Jacob for ever;
> and of his kingdom (βασιλείας) there will be
> no end. (Luke 1:32–3)

> To you is born this day in the city of David a Savior (σωτήρ),
> who is Christ the Lord (Χριστός κύριος). (Luke 2:11)

> As my Father has appointed a kingdom (βασιλείαν) for me so
> do I appoint for you that you may eat and drink at my table
> in my kingdom, and sit on twelve thrones judging the twelve
> tribes of Israel. (Luke 22:29–30)[14]

At Jesus' trial the meaning of the title 'Messiah' was made clear for
Pilate (Luke 23:2). Moreover, Jesus did not deny being a king, though
any ambition for an earthly kingdom was dashed at the crucifixion.
Immediately following the soldiers' taunt, 'If you are King of the Jews,
save yourself!', Luke inserted the inscription on the cross: 'This is the
King of the Jews' (Luke 23:37–8).

Would a Roman, whose ultimate authority was the emperor, have had
the background, education, or patience to understand the non-political
nuances in Luke's majestic Christology?[15]

4. The ending of Acts

The enigmatic ending of Acts raises two questions for the critical reader:
(1) Does Luke's ending support a presentation of Christianity as a politically harmless movement? If Paul had been judged innocent and released,
Luke ignored this outcome which might have helped settle the question
of Christian political harmlessness. (2) Does the ending speak against the
Roman authorities? In spite of Paul's political innocence Luke seems
to hint that Paul has been executed (Acts 20:22–5, 38). In order to
deal with these issues we must raise again the familiar question: why
did Luke cease writing before telling the reader the outcome of Paul's
trial?

> Several solutions have been proposed:
> (1) Luke died before he could finish his work.[16]
> (2) The original ending which reported Paul's martyrdom has been
>   removed.[17]
> (3) Luke intended to write a third volume to Theophilus.[18]
> (4) Luke ceased writing because he knew no more.[19]

(5) . Luke chose not to continue his narrative even though he knew Paul's fate.

In the final analysis, the first four options are not very compelling. Even if they do solve the mystery, they also leave us mired in ambiguity about Paul's fate and Luke's intentions. They do not lead us very far toward resolving the question of Luke's political apologetic (with respect to Paul, Christianity, or the empire) which may be implied by the ending. It is only the last of these options that renders a plausible basis for resolving the problem and sheds additional light on Luke's political perspective.

Even though Luke knew the outcome of Paul's trial, he made a decision not to continue his narrative. Three reasons are generally advanced for this: (1) Luke has completed his literary task; (2) since Luke's readers knew the outcome of Paul's trial (whether release [2a] or execution [2b]), it was needless for him to report it; (3) Luke was too embarrassed by the denouement of Paul's life to continue the story.

(1) In reporting the history of the church up to the arrival of Paul in Rome, Luke has completed his literary task.[20] That Luke stopped his narrative with Paul in Rome is consonant with the literary design of his second volume. The program of Acts 1:8 — the triumphal progress of the gospel from Jerusalem to Rome — has been achieved. Bengel was elegant in his declaration: 'Victoria Verbi Dei, Paulus Romae, Apex Evangelii, Actorum Finis.'[21] Yet, without denying either Luke's literary skill or the importance of ending his two volumes with Paul in Rome, one needs to consider the probability (based on hints of Paul's death in Acts 20:22—5, 38) that Luke and his readers knew the next chapter in the life of Paul.

(2a) Perhaps Luke's readers knew that Paul was released from house-arrest. One is led inevitably to ask why Luke did not add another paragraph or two which would have reported Paul's release, vindicating the apostle and the imperial government?

Answers to this question tend to be more psychological than exegetical. K. Lake proposed that the release of Paul (because his accusers did not bring their case to Rome within the 'two-year' time limit) was 'disappointing to Luke from the point of view of Christian apologetic.'[22] It is difficult to imagine how a statement about Paul's release would have been disappointing. If one assumes the traditional view of Luke's apologetic, announcement of Paul's release would have shown that Rome continued to be impartial toward Paul (and the Christian community).[23]

The parallels between Luke's presentation of the trials of Jesus and Paul might suggest that Luke would rather not make too much of Paul's superior civil position. Jesus the peasant was quickly tried and executed as a common criminal; Paul the citizen, on the other hand, was investigated, treated fairly by the authorities, and released.[24]

There is a slender thread of evidence that suggests a slightly less psychological solution. Miles and Trompf conclude that Luke's account of Paul's shipwreck

> amounted to a theological *tour de force* in the eyes of ancient readers. Paul was put to the test by forces and exigencies [shipwreck and snakebite] far more dreaded than the requirements of a human law court, and since [by overcoming these tests] he had been found guiltless, what need was there to recount the outcome of his appeal?[25]

Even this solution, however, demands some 'mind reading' of Luke's intention in not mentioning Paul's fate.

(2b) Perhaps Luke and his readers knew that Paul's trial ended in the martyrdom of the apostle. If Luke was attempting to present Rome at its best or to preserve Paul's innocence, then it is not surprising that he has suppressed such an ending. That Luke chose not to report Paul's fate at the hands of Rome may indicate how cautious, even overly cautious, he was in presenting a favorable picture of the empire, for even if Paul had been executed during Nero's reign, Luke's readers would not have seen this as a disgrace for Paul or a miscarriage of Roman justice.[26] Hanson points out that many honourable and eminent men such as Seneca and Burrus 'had been put to death by the capricious and suspicious Nero ... [Luke] may even have meant to make the point that in normal circumstances when angry tyrants do not interfere with the course of justice, Christianity expects, and receives, fair treatment at the hands of the Roman Government.'[27]

(3) There is one final resolution to the problem, not without a psychological component, yet with sufficient evidence to render it the most attractive of alternatives. In his study of Peter, Oscar Cullmann offered the following conclusion based on an examination of 1 Clement 5: 'When Clement ... writes that Peter had to suffer "on account of unrighteous jealousy," and Paul "on account of jealousy and strife", ... this in the context of our letter can only mean that they were *victims of jealousy from persons who counted themselves members of the Christian Church.*'[28] According to Cullmann, the way Clement and Paul use the terms 'envy' and 'strife' points to fratricide;[29] Paul considered himself to be in danger 'among false brethren.'[30] S. Wilson finds supporting evidence for this conclusion from his study of the Pastoral Epistles. 2 Timothy 1:15 may hint

that 'all those in Asia' not only 'turned away' from Paul, but also conspired in his imprisonment and death. 2 Tim.4.9f. refers to the desertion of Paul by most of his travelling companions and v. 16 claims that 'at my first defense no one took my part; all deserted me'. Is it possible that this reflects what Luke knew when he wrote Acts, namely that there were Christians who had a hand in his death, either by positive action or passive compliance?[31]

It could well be that Luke did not continue his story of Paul because he was embarrassed by the ending. Luke's emphasis — one could say over-emphasis — on the treachery of the Jews leads one to think that perhaps 'he protests too much.' More than one scholar has seen that Luke has circumspectly identified 'the Jews from Asia,' whose accusations led to Paul's arrest and trial (Acts 21:27), as Jews and not Jewish-Christians.[32] Perhaps Luke, embarrassed by what he knows to be the truth about Paul's demise — that Jewish-Christians from Asia had a hand in Paul's arrest, trial, and execution — has glossed this over by implicating *only* 'Jews from Asia.'[33] Finally, one might ask why Luke has included the detail about Paul's nephew being privy to a plot to ambush and kill Paul (Acts 23:16). Could it be that this 'son of Paul's sister' was a Jewish-Christian, yet chose not to remain part of a conspiracy (of Jews and Jewish-Christians) against Paul?

Whatever the validity of these reasons, whether Paul was martyred in Rome[34] is still, and probably always will be, a tantalizing historical question. Both of our primary sources, Luke and Clement, equivocate about this. Though they may have known the details regarding Paul's death, they have attempted to identify Jews and/or Jewish-Christians, rather than the Romans, as the miscreants. Luke's silence about Paul's fate not only indicates his embarrassment about the identity of the real villains, it was also a means of preserving his positive assessment of the Roman empire.

To return to the two questions with which we began this section, I must conclude that a Roman reader would not have been much impressed by such an ambiguous end to Paul's case. (1) Does the ending support the view that Luke has presented Christianity as a politically harmless movement? A curious official might have searched the court records for the resolution of Paul's case; a lazy official might have concluded that Christian politics were still suspect. (2) Does Luke's ambiguity speak against the Roman authorities? A Christian reader would not necessarily have concluded from the ending that Roman jurisprudence was malevolent. Paul was alive, relatively free to pursue his interests, and waiting for the Jews (not the Romans) to press their case against him. The one certain truth about the ending of Acts is that it cannot be construed as anti-Roman.

5. Conclusion

Before we consider additional Lucan passages that have been traditionally interpreted as anti-Roman, we shall conclude this section by noting a few remaining items in Luke—Acts that must have raised questions in the minds of Roman officials (if such were intended to read this work) about Christian political loyalties.

The annunciation to Mary —'he has put down the mighty from their thrones' (Luke 1:52) — is hardly a pious statement, nor is the biblical text (Luke 4:18—19) which Jesus read to the congregation at Nazareth, nor is Jesus' declaration, 'I came to cast fire upon the earth; and would that it were already kindled! ... Do you think that I have come to give peace on earth? No, I tell you, but rather division' (Luke 12:49, 51). These words of Jesus could not have been more opposed to the imperial goals of peace and harmony. Only with great difficulty can one conclude that a non-Christian Roman reader would have construed these messages as politically harmless.

In the Acts of the Apostles, the disciples declare that they must serve God rather than men (Acts 5:29). Hearing this, Gamaliel cautions the council about the apostles in a curious manner by comparing them with two revolutionary groups of the recent past.[35] Later, Paul is identified (wrongly, of course) by Claudius Lysias as a leader of the *sicarii* (Acts 21:38). Furthermore, the apostles 'did not cease teaching and preaching Jesus as the Christ' and Paul preached 'the kingdom of God' and taught about 'the Lord Jesus Christ' openly in Rome (Acts 5:42; 28:31).

If one of the purposes of Luke's narrative was to bring an *apologia pro ecclesia* to a Roman reader, he might have been as careful to skew his sources in a non-political way as he was in reworking his material in a pro-Roman direction. Before taking up this latter theme, however, we must look at those passages in Luke—Acts in which Rome is unfavorably presented.

B. Did Luke present an unfavorable picture of Roman authority?

In the previous section I pointed to several passages that would have raised doubts in the Roman mind about Christian political loyalties. I have also

suggested that we come closer to understanding the *raison d'être* of Luke's
political presentation if we infer that Luke, like every New Testament
author, was addressing the church, not Rome. If, as I am convinced,
Luke's message was pro-Roman, then we must consider any evidence to
the contrary.

E. Franklin raises the issue of Luke's presentation of Roman authority
and concludes that Luke depicts imperial power as sometimes capricious,
sometimes harsh, and occasionally corrupt; nevertheless, 'Luke's purpose
seems to be to present additional material regarding Jewish perversity
rather than to make a defense of Roman practices.'[36] Franklin mentions
several Lucan passages unfavorable to Rome; I shall add to his list and
draw some preliminary conclusions about the evidence.

(1)   Luke 13:1. Pilate ordered the slaughter of Galileans.
(2)   Luke 23:13–25. Pilate gave way to Jewish pressure at Jesus' trial.
(3)   Luke 19:41–4; 21:5–36; 23:27–31. The Romans destroyed Jerusalem.
(4)   Acts 16:19–40. After Paul and Silas were accused by Greeks of
      Philippi of disturbing the peace and advocating unlawful customs,
      colonial magistrates ($\sigma\tau\rho\alpha\tau\eta\gamma o\acute{\iota}$) ordered them to be beaten and
      jailed. Having discovered their Roman citizenship, they apologized
      to Paul and Silas and asked them to leave the city.
(5)   Acts 17:1–10. Again, nervous city authorities ($\pi o\lambda\iota\tau\acute{\alpha}\rho\chi\alpha\varsigma$) sent
      Paul and Silas from the free city of Thessalonica, this time
      because the Jews falsely accused them of 'acting against the
      decrees of Caesar, saying that there is another king, Jesus.'
(6)   Acts 21:37–40. The tribune Lysias, having discovered Paul to be
      no revolutionary, had Paul remanded in custody. Lysias remitted
      Paul's case to the governor, Felix.
(7)   Acts 24:26–7. Felix kept Paul in prison hoping to obtain a
      bribe.
(8)   Acts 25:11. Paul's appeal to Caesar suggests 'that Paul by no
      means had confidence in [the trial's] final outcome (Acts 25:25).
      The whole account of Paul's appeal to Rome abounds in incon-
      sistencies. Rome accepts Paul's innocence, yet she is not prepared
      to act on it but rather treats him as a threat to the peace and one
      who might be well sacrificed in order to procure security and
      establish Jewish favor.'[37]

It is certainly true that in Luke–Acts the local magistrates appear weak
and indecisive at times. Yet Luke consistently presents these magistrates
against the backdrop of (1) jealous Jews who constantly pressure the
authorities to act against Christians and (2) a durable imperial legal system

that transcends local administrative waffling. None of these episodes depicts Rome as an enemy of Christianity. At worst, it can be said that the civil authorities succumbed to Jewish pressure; most often, they acted out of ignorance; and at best, the Roman judicial system protected the apostles from the chaos and caprice of an unruly mob. To say this, however, is hardly sufficient exegesis. Therefore, I shall return to investigate each episode, except the first, in the next two chapters.

For the moment a closer look at the difficult passage in Luke 13 is in order. Perhaps the Evangelist has presented a piece of traditional material which attests to the vile nature of Pilate. Aside from this passage nothing is known of the incident. The only possible, but unlikely, episode to which Luke 13:1 might refer is Pilate's furious attack on suspected Samaritan rebels on Mount Gerizim, an act for which he paid with his job.[38] This incident, however, did not occur until after the crucifixion of Jesus.

It is clear that in Luke 13:1 the Evangelist has something of importance to say about Jewish—Roman relations during Jesus' ministry. Those scholars intent in finding direct links between Jesus and the Zealots point to this passage as evidence of Jesus' anti-Roman attitude.[39] However, when the passage is taken in its wider context it becomes apparent that Pilate is not the subject of discussion; rather, it is the Jews with whom Jesus is concerned. The pericopes that follow – the parable of the fig tree, the healing of the deformed woman, and the householder who excludes all workers of iniquity from the messianic banquet – point to the tragic consequence of rejecting the gospel message. With Luke 13: 34—5 we are brought by means of a summary back to the conflict between the Jews and Rome. Jerusalem, which has killed the prophets sent to her, is forsaken. Those unfortunate Galileans are only a portent of what is in store for the nation; those who provoked Pilate's wrath will yet spread their infectious disease of revolution and bring ultimate doom to all other Galileans if the nation does not repent. Likewise, for those who dwell in Jerusalem, God is preparing a judgment and it matters not whether it comes by sword (13:1) or accident (13:4). The vehicle of destruction is unimportant; what matters is that by her rejection of Jesus the doom of the nation is now scheduled on the divine calendar.

It is doubtful that Luke has included this pericope as part of an anti-Roman polemic. Rather, Luke 13:1—5 must be seen as one of several prophecies which describe the consequences for an unrepentant and unbelieving people. What is only hinted at in this oracle and in 19:41—4 – that Rome has been designated as God's agent of retributive justice – is clearly presented in Luke's version of the 'Synoptic Apocalypse.'[40] As we

shall see in the rest of this book, whatever material in Luke—Acts that is
unfavorable to Rome is far from a sustained anti-Roman polemic such as
one finds in 4 Esdras, the Sibylline Oracles (Book VIII), or John's Apocalypse. Rather, in reporting the encounters between representatives of the
Christian movement and the Roman empire, Luke has often glossed over
the negative perspective regarding the empire contained in his sources
while actively promoting a positive representation of Roman rule.

C. Luke's positive view of imperial authority

Luke is not negative nor even neutral toward the empire. He has high
regard for the imperial government and for those who administer it.
Throughout Luke—Acts, the Evangelist has done his best to modify his
sources in order to sculpt the virtues of the empire in high relief. This
modification is, of course, most evident in the Third Gospel for we have
Mark and, to some extent, Q as controls; it is more difficult to make such
a comparative study of Luke's second volume. Nevertheless, in the analysis
of the following five passages of the Third Gospel, I shall refer occasionally
to Luke's pro-Roman perspective as it occurs woven throughout the fabric
of both volumes.

1. The decree of Augustus and the birth of Jesus (Luke 2:1—5)

It is not incidental that Luke connects the birth of Jesus and the beginning
of his ministry with Augustus and Tiberius, Quirinius and Pilate. From its
very beginning the Christian movement was rooted firmly in the matrix of
the empire. Just as firmly, according to Luke, the movement had its roots
in the Old Testament. While Luke styles the annunciation, birth, and
response to the coming of Jesus after the Old Testament, the *imperium*
provides the backdrop against which these events take place.[41]

We have already noted how the piling up of kingly titles in the birth
narrative was not likely to evoke a positive response from a Roman official;
this could hardly have been part of an *apologia pro ecclesia*. However, a
Christian reading this material would appreciate both the glorious titles
given the babe of Bethlehem and the political and social perspective
proffered by Luke.

Whether or not Luke was dependent on sources for these opening
verses, there is at least one point in the birth narrative where the hand of
the Evangelist clearly may be seen (exclusive of his introduction): Luke
2:1—5.[42] W. L. Knox has shown that this passage is the first of several in
the Gospel where Luke's excellent Greek shines 'like a good deed in a

naughty world,' for with verse 6 the narrative immediately lapses back into a 'riot of parataxis and semitic pronouns.'[43]

Luke has not simply demonstrated a sophisticated syntax, but, more importantly, he has announced one of his fundamental themes: God's plan for salvation is being worked out in concert with the continuing history of the Roman empire. Caesar Augustus had made a dramatic world-wide edict which provided the proper circumstances for the birth of the Messiah.

Scholars have long been troubled by Luke's historical blunder with respect to the census.[44] Our non-Lucan sources mention neither a 'world-wide' census ordered by Augustus nor a census in Palestine during the reign of Herod the Great. Nor is there evidence that Quirinius was legate of Syria during Herod's lifetime. All attempts to reconcile the Lucan anachronism with what we otherwise know of Roman history have reached a frustrating stalemate — frustrating, because Luke proposes to render an orderly account, and indeed he maintains a chronological interest throughout his writing.[45] Without new epigraphical or textual evidence, the deadlock will continue.[46]

Several scholars have recently suggested that Luke may have intentionally, or unintentionally, distorted the chronology in order to link the census of AD 6 with Jesus' birth. Those who propose an *intentional* distortion also propose a source behind Luke 2:1–5. According to H. Braunert these verses were originally the product of a Christian Zealot group which connected the birth of Jesus with the rise of their own patriotic movement; the census provoked the tax revolt led by Judas the Galilean.[47]

Building on this foundation W. Grundmann states that 'Joseph's journey [to Bethlehem] signals the rejection of the Zealot way which opposes the imperial decree.'[48] H. Moehring provides the mortar which bonds this anti-Zealot message with Luke's political apologetic purpose.

> By underlining the obedience of Jesus' family and the Christian community while openly confessing their Jewish origin Luke may have intended to claim that the Christians are the true Jews even in the Roman legal sense. As the true Jews who have never been involved in any rebellion against Rome or any other subversive activity the Christians should be accorded the privileges of a *religio licita* ... [49]

While I agree with Moehring that after AD 70 there would have been some concern among early Christians not to be associated with the Zealot party, I would turn his conclusion slightly. Luke's message *to the church* is to follow the example of Jesus' parents. Pay taxes to whom taxes are due thus avoiding any suspicions about Christian loyalty.

Raymond Brown has recently written that Luke *unintentionally* made the historical error; '... the use of the census to explain the presence of Joseph and Mary at Bethlehem is a Lucan device based on a confused memory.'[50] Luke knew of two troubled endings to Herodian reigns. At the death of Herod the Great (4 BC) the Jews protested the giving of Judea to Archelaus, and when Archelaus was forced to abdicate in AD 6, some Jews protested the census ordered by Quirinius. Luke simply was confused about these two troubling transition periods.

Why, then, did Luke include this garbled piece of history? Perhaps it was to shift the drama from Nazareth to Bethlehem. Brown thinks Luke surely could have found a less complicated way to do this, though there is a certain straightforward and compelling simplicity to a 'world-wide' edict. An alternative Lucan motive, according to Brown, may have been to contrast the advent of the *pax Augusta* with that of *pax Christi*.

In 29 BC Octavian put an end to the internecine wars that had ravaged the Mediterranean world. Upon his glorious return to Rome the senate proclaimed him 'Augustus' and moved to erect an altar to *pax Augusta* in the Campus Martius.[51] Virgil could exult over the 'baby boy' who, having received 'the life of gods', reigned 'o'er a world at peace.'[52] It was only fitting that such a man be deemed 'savior of the whole world.'[53] Brown concludes, 'It can scarcely be accidental that Luke's description of the birth of Jesus presents an implicit challenge to this imperial propaganda, not by denying the imperial ideals, but by claiming that the real peace of the world was brought about by Jesus.'[54] Yet one must wonder to what end Luke would devise such a challenge. Marshall correctly notes that 'such language was in common currency rather than ... necessarily contrived in opposition to imperial claims.'[55]

One could read the material in quite another way. Augustus had a part to play in God's plan for salvation. His edict set the plan in motion, Jesus the Messiah was born appropriately in Bethlehem, and the angels sang the doxology that the *pax Augusta* was completed (complemented) by the *pax Christi*. 'Peace on earth' was God's good news brought to people of good will through the birth of a baby boy.[56]

Unlike Josephus, who maintained a negative view of the census and its consequences, Luke subscribed to a positive view of the edict.[57] The decree of Caesar had led to a legitimate ordering of a previously chaotic government. The locus of this passage, πρώτη ('the first enrollment'), indicates a qualitative contrast between the condition in Palestine during Jesus' lifetime and the state of affairs prior to the new order.[58] Organized

government had at last come to Judea; Joseph, testifying to the legitimacy
and authority of that government, went willingly to be enrolled at Bethlehem. The beginning of a new order for the holy land under Caesar Augustus
also marks the beginning of a new order for the holy people under Jesus
Christ. Luke had no intention of positing an affinity between the rise of
the Zealots and the birth of Jesus nor of challenging the ideal of *pax
Augusta*. Rather, the 'world-wide' decree which Luke records united the
world under a universal politic of peace and it provided a fitting birth
announcement for him who would found a universal religion of peace.

2. The preaching of John the Baptist to the Jewish proletariat and the representatives of Rome (Luke 3:10–14)

In Luke's account of the preaching of John the Baptist, three representative groups are present in the wilderness to hear the Baptist's message:
'the crowds' – the peasant class, 'the tax-collectors' – Jewish agents of
the Roman empire, and 'the soldiers' – guardians of imperial order.[59]

It is uncertain whether Luke has derived 3:10–14 from a source or
has added the material himself.[60] The vocabulary is sufficiently Hellenistic,
and the groups addressed a matter of such concern for Luke, that it would
be easy to see a Lucan interpolation here. The Jewish proletariat, pro-
Roman loyalists, and low-ranking army officials may well have reflected
the constituency of Luke's own church. This would have been a message
of historical interest to them. Each group of pilgrims was receptive to
John's message of ethics and repentance; each was being prepared for
Jesus' ministry and Luke's church. For us, this passage invites a discussion
of how Luke treats these groups in his writing.

a. The crowds (οἱ ὄχλοι)

Throughout his Gospel, Luke has carefully distinguished the masses from
their leaders. The multitudes, expecting a Messiah, have sought after
Jesus, welcomed him, and followed him.[61] Jesus willingly taught them,
welcomed their company, dined with them, and healed their diseases.[62]
Jesus evoked praises to God from the crowds which put the leaders to
shame and made them fearful of the crowd's growing attachment to
Jesus.[63] Finally, even though the peasants seem temporarily to be swayed
by their rulers to rise against Jesus,[64] they are quick to realize their
mistake after the crucifixion and return home penitently 'beating their
breasts.'[65]

It is obvious that the disciples of Jesus are drawn from the peasant
class; they, too, are regularly rebuked by the Pharisees for infractions

of the law and for refusal to practice an ascetic life.[66] In the Acts of the Apostles, Peter and John are perceived by the rulers as being from the illiterate and ignorant masses: ὅτι ἄνθρωποι ἀγράμματοί εἰσιν καὶ ἰδιῶται.[67]

It is not surprising, then, to find Luke deviating from his source to have John the Baptist address himself not to the Pharisees and Sadducees,[68] but to the crowds, for it is they who heed the message of John and are baptized.[69]

The message which John delivers to the crowds is a condensation of Old Testament ethics.[70] To share one's food and clothing with the needy is a fulfillment of the ethical proclamation of the prophets. Even the lowest of Palestinian Jewry may have a part in that prophetic tradition. But Luke, through John, does not stop with the 'Sons of Abraham.' The representatives of Rome are invited by John the Baptist to join in the spirit of the Augustan age. In the preaching of the Baptist, as in the birth narrative, Luke has woven together strands of Old Testament and Augustan ethics.

b. The tax-collectors (οἱ τελῶναι)

For Luke the tax-collectors form a middle link in the chain of lower social classes in Palestine.

The annals of ancient history contain sufficient evidence that the Roman system of taxation which developed during the Republic was at best inefficient and irregular, and at worst abusive and illegal.[71] While it seems clear from the literature that 'only the most gross cases of illegal requisition and bribery' have come to our notice, one can assume by the very nature of the tax system that smaller, but more constant, abuses plagued the Palestinian peasant.[72]

The local governor might have been conscientious and orderly, but his hands were tied when dealing with the less than scrupulous *publicani* for two reasons. First, it was the governor's responsibility to raise the tribute required of him by Rome. In order to accomplish this, he had to rely on the productivity of the tax-gatherers. Second, the *publicani* were not civil servants but part of a vast private business enterprise with headquarters in Rome. To challenge the practice of a local publican could lead to a confrontation with Rome's most influential citizens. A provincial magistrate might find it difficult to deal firmly with so powerful a business on which his own position of authority relied.

When a province was assigned its tribute, bids were let for the collection of the tax. Needless to say, the highest bidder won the contract which included the tax assessment plus local administrative expenses incurred by the governor. The tax-gathering companies would then pass the cost of doing business (profits for shareholders, salaries for tax-collectors and company managers) plus the tax assessed to the local peasant.[73]

According to G. H. Stevenson this

> extravagant system ... aroused deep resentment among the provincials, ... for too large a part of the yield of taxation went to the *publicani* and unscrupulous governors. It is probable, too, that the burden of taxation was unevenly distributed and fell too often on the wrong shoulders. What was wanted was that the *publicani* should be dispensed with or rigidly supervised, that the governors should be prevented from enriching themselves at the cost of the provincials, and that taxation should be imposed as equitably as possible. In all these respects excellent work was done in the reign of Augustus.[74]

The Augustan reforms did seem to hold out hope for the provincials. Already, in 44 BC, Julius Caesar ordered the abolition of the farming of direct taxes (*tributum soli, tributum capitis*) in Palestine.[75] Under the Principate, these taxes were to be collected by state officials appointed by the governor. Customs and other indirect taxes, on the other hand, continued to be leased out to tax farmers. In both cases, attempts were made by provincial governors, with the encouragement of Rome, to curb intimidation, rapacity, and other abuses which tempted the tax-collector.[76]

Since the tax-collectors who heard John the Baptist were in the company of soldiers, they were probably agents of the procurator, Pilate.[77] That they, like the peasants, 'also came to be baptized' would indicate that they were Jews, although hated by their countrymen, who classified them with sinners, harlots, gentiles, and robbers.[78]

Luke reflects in John's preaching the challenge of the Augustan reforms: 'Collect no more than is appointed you!' This is not only a command to act morally, but a charge to the publicans to let their dealings be reflective and supportive of the high ideals of the Augustan age.

The story of Zacchaeus reveals Luke's familiarity with the Roman system of taxation in Palestine, for he correctly placed the scene in Jericho, one of the eleven district headquarters for the collection of Roman taxes.[79] Residing in Jericho as the chief tax-collector (ἀρχιτελώνης), Zacchaeus is the object of scorn not only from the Pharisees, but from the peasantry, in whose eyes this agent of the Roman government is 'a sinner.'[80] Yet Zacchaeus repents in Jesus' presence, as his underlings did before John the Baptist. As a word of caution to those who look down on the despised tax-collector, the crowd is reminded of the message preached by the Baptist.

This Jewish tax-collector, even though he stands in direct relation to the *imperium*, is still a 'son of Abraham.'

God is able to raise up the lowly 'stones' of society to work out his purposes,[81] and so tax-collectors along with the crowds are baptized. The soldiers must wait until 'the time of the church'.

c. The soldiers (οἱ στρατευόμενοι)

The group held in least regard by the Jewish nation was also present at the preaching of the Baptist: soldiers on active duty.[82]

Luke does not depreciate the contribution of the army, any more than that of the tax-collectors, toward government in Palestine. John the Baptist did not call for vocational change, but simply the ethical practice of one's calling. Unlike the Fourth Gospel and the book of Revelation, Luke presents the Roman military in a positive light.[83] Officers are especially commended for their fairness and good judgment as well as their unique contribution to the dissemination of the gospel. Throughout Luke—Acts several centurions are portrayed favorably: it was a centurion who loved the nation of Israel, who made the final proclamation of Jesus' innocence, who became the first non-Jewish Christian, who prevented the scourging of Paul, who saved Paul from an assassination plot of the Jews, who escorted Paul safely from Jerusalem to Caesarea, and who at last brought Paul and his message to the capital of the Roman world.[84]

Among higher-ranking Romans, the governor of Cyprus, Sergius Paulus, was friendly toward the apostle and his preaching; at Philippi Paul received a public apology from the town magistrates for their precipitous judgment; at Corinth, Seneca's brother and proconsul of Achaea, Annaeus Gallio, refused to listen to accusations against Paul; at Ephesus, Paul was begged by the Asiarchs not to venture among an angry mob; and in Jerusalem a tribune, Claudius Lysias, found no offence in Paul's preaching and protected him with a cadre of soldiers.[85] Moreover, the Roman commander-in-chief stationed in Judea found both Jesus and Paul innocent of charges brought against them.[86]

The deportment and good discipline of the Roman army is not called into question, but proves to be a great asset to the mission of the church. Again, Luke places on the lips of the Baptist a message which reflects Augustan ideals: do not extort from the populace;[87] be content with your wages.[88] The soldiers have every reason to be prepared by the preaching of John, for they will eventually have an important function to perform with respect to the preservation and growth of the gospel message.

The Lucan narrative of the preaching mission of John the Baptist allows us to see how the Third Evangelist perceived the proletariat of Palestine: peasants, tax-collectors, and soldiers. Jesus stands with (and the Jewish leaders against) all three groups, for all will share in the growth of the Christian church. Luke's message to the church is that in the past John the Baptist preached to Jews, 'half-Jews,' and pagans. Now the church must assume John's perspective and receive Romans as well as Jews; salvation is available for all levels of society. In typically Lucan fashion, particularly in the early chapters of the Third Gospel, the tradition of the Old Testament and the spirit of the Augustan age are woven together.[89] To the Jews, Luke has John the Baptist preach the heart of the prophets' ethical concerns; likewise, John reminds the servants of Rome of the Augustan reforms.

3. Jesus and the centurion: two authorities (Luke 7:1–10)

With this Q pericope Luke has taken up the theme of 'authority.' In the dialogue between Jesus and the centurion (through his friends), Luke compared two kinds of authority: the centurion had imperial authority to control earthly events, while Jesus possessed divine authority over the spirit world. Prior to this encounter Luke had mentioned the realm of Jesus' authority. After Jesus' sermon at Capernaum the congregation was 'astonished at his teaching, for his *word* was with *authority*' (Luke 4:32). And in the same synagogue, after exorcizing a demon, the people again responded, 'What is this *word*? For with *authority* and power he commands unclean spirits, and they come out' (Luke 4:36). While the empire has authority to move men, Jesus moves the spirits.[90]

Matthew's terse version of the episode of the centurion's servant appears closer to the Q tradition than does Luke 7:1–10. The centurion had visited Jesus and asked him to heal his sick servant. Following a short discussion on authority, Jesus offered to heal the servant by the authority of his word and because of the faith of the centurion.

Luke has modified the Q account primarily by expanding the presentation of the authoritative position and good character of the centurion.[91] Not only was the gentile soldier an officer in the auxiliary army of Herod Antipas,[92] but Luke indicates that he was wealthy enough to build a synagogue and that he was stationed in or near Capernaum.[93] Luke seems also to imply that the centurion was not a God-fearer or proselyte, for when such a title is applicable he uses it.[94] Luke's source did not indicate the centurion's place of citizenship, but this does not deter the Third Evangelist from presenting the centurion to his readers as a model of

Roman citizenry stationed in the provinces — syncretistic in belief, cosmopolitan in outlook, and friendly toward the quaint Palestinian natives. Moreover, the centurion's disposition fits well the Roman attitude toward religion in the early empire. A. D. Nock and others have pointed to the revival in traditional Greek and Roman religions which was encouraged by Augustus. The Augustan policy not only intended to restore worship of the traditional deities, but also to regulate ruler-worship, to revive the older provincial cults, and to rebuild temples that had fallen into ruin. That the centurion should build a synagogue marks that soldier as an exemplar of the Augustan religious restoration.[95]

Most commentators are content to say that the centurion was a gentile. Sherwin-White states that this centurion could not have been a Roman soldier because 'Capernaum was in the heart of the tetrarchy of Herod. Galilee was never part of a Roman province until the death of Agrippa I in AD 44. The centurion must be a soldier of Herod ... '[96] This ignores the fact that Galilee was once part of the kingdom of Herod the Great who ruled with the aid of a Roman-staffed army. Upon inheriting the tetrarchy, Antipas also accepted Roman leadership of this army.[97]

There can be no doubt that Luke had a Roman officer in mind. In 7:4 he used the Latinism, $\check{α}ξιός ἐστιν ᾧ παρέξῃ τοῦτο$, which is scarce in the New Testament and used primarily in connection with Roman authorities.[98] In verse 8 Luke adds the passive participle $τασσόμενος$ to Q. Not only was the centurion 'under authority,' but he had been 'placed under authority' by appointment.[99] Finally, even with the good pay of a centurion, it is unlikely that a provincial member of the auxiliary would have amassed enough money to build a synagogue, nor is it likely that a provincial gentile soldier would be so inclined to help the Jews of his region, whereas a Roman from a wealthy family could have been moved to do so.

Perhaps a word is in order about the troops serving Antipas. There was a qualitative difference between the Roman legions made up, at least nominally, of Roman citizens, and provincial auxiliaries made up of local recruits. At the foot-soldier level, Herod's army would have consisted of Jews and non-Jews from the lowest classes of Galilee.[100] The situation among the officers, however, was somewhat different. Officers of centurion rank and above were, with few exceptions, Roman citizens appointed to their posts by the emperor.[101] But would a Roman centurion be serving in an auxiliary army and could he afford to be so generous? The answer to both questions is yes. In their normal rotation of duty, each centurion was required to serve an occasional term in the auxiliary forces.[102] The centurion whom Luke had in mind was assigned to the army of Herod, but still owed his full allegiance to the legate of Syria, his closest Roman commander-in-chief. We cannot doubt the wealth of this centurion for not only would he have been well paid, but many came from well-to-do families.[103]

Luke presented the centurion as the finest example of Roman military personnel. The Third Evangelist has emphasized three imperial virtues: friendship, respect for authority, and piety.[104] He was loving toward his servant and, like any good Roman citizen, he adapted well to his foreign surroundings, making friends of the local leaders. In their eyes this gentile was 'worthy ... for he loves our nation and built us a synagogue' (Luke 7:4–5).

Traditional scholarship has made much of the 'humility' of the centurion before Jesus. Perhaps a better adjective in the context of this dialogue would be 'respect,' a mutual respect between Jesus and the centurion. On the one hand, Jesus 'marveled' at all the authority by which the empire, through her designee, can control men. Likewise, the centurion stood in awe of Jesus' authority over the spirit world. 'Just give the order and my servant will get well,'[105] reflects the centurion's respect for Jesus' *auctoritas*, that power by which he compels the spirits to obey his will. For Luke's reader this means that the representatives of the empire have rightful authority over the earthly realm, while the church, through the word of Jesus which continues in the church, has authority over the unseen, but powerful, world of spirits.

Finally, the Third Evangelist has discovered in this old Palestinian tradition a prototype which spoke to the events of his own day. More clearly than Matthew, he emphasized that the Roman citizen was capable of great faith which transcended both time and space: 'not even in Israel have I found such faith' (Luke 7:9). While *auctoritas* is the compelling power of a superior, *pietas* is the expression of respect for authority by a subordinate.[106] The centurion possesses the authority of a commanding officer; he also is a man 'placed under authority' and therefore bound to the higher authority by his oath of loyalty. Not even in Israel is there such potential for piety that transcends even the highest of earthly authorities.

This story of the friendship, authority and piety of the centurion in Luke's Gospel prefigures the account of the conversion of Cornelius in Luke's second volume.[107] Jesus, living under the law, was hindered from coming into the home of the Roman centurion, whereas Peter, free from the law, can be sent by God[108] to have full communion with the centurion Cornelius who, like the centurion of the Gospel, was 'a devout man who feared God ..., and was well spoken of by the whole Jewish nation.'[109]

While the centurion of the Gospel recognized Jesus' authority at a distance, and Jesus commented on his great piety, Cornelius demonstrated his great respect for the divine authority which Peter represented by prostrating himself before Peter.[110] And just as the centurion of the Gospel was the first of the gentiles to receive a benefit by the word of the Lord, so now in Luke's church Roman officials may be received into full fellowship.

4. The payment of tribute to Caesar (Luke 20:20–6)

In view of Luke's pro-Roman perspective it is not surprising that he related this episode from his Marcan source with few alterations. Most of his changes were designed to heighten the treachery of the Jewish leaders. The contrast between them and the centurion could not have been greater. Explicitly, the leaders send 'spies' to trap Jesus into an 'either or' (God *or* Caesar) answer; Jesus, of course, wisely responded, 'both and' (God *and* Caesar). Luke continues the 'tribute' motif by connecting the spies' conniving question to the perjurious accusation brought by the Sanhedrin to Pilate (23:2). Implicitly, Luke's introduction indicates that the question of tribute was being debated behind the scenes by the Jewish leadership. They were disingenuous not only toward Jesus, but toward Rome as well.

The thrust of Jesus' actual response – whether it was pro-Roman (Bornkamm, Grundmann, Ellis) or anti-Roman (Brandon) – is of secondary importance to this study.[111] What concerns us is what *Luke* thought of this episode and how it fits with the rest of his material on Christian–Roman relations. Luke, like his Christian contemporaries, was not as concerned with separating Jesus from the Zealot mission as he was in promoting an accord between the church and the state. And like his Christian and non-Christian contemporaries, Luke knew that earthly authority was derived from God's authority;[112] obedience to Caesar, therefore, was also obedience to divinely ordained authority.[113] Ellis rightly concludes that for Luke, Jesus' answer 'becomes an abiding principle for the Church's relation to the state.'[114]

Some recent commentators have presented a rather confused interpretation of this passage. Danker, for example, holding on to the traditional view that Luke has presented an *apologia pro ecclesia*, states: 'Luke knows that the identification of Jesus as a king has raised eyebrows. This story should clear the air. "Down with the establishment" is not his theme song. There is nothing wrong with the establishment as such.'[115]

Jesus' political innocence is not an issue here; rather the church is reminded about its duty to 'the establishment.' A Roman official would have been only mildly impressed with this episode. Naturally, people are to pay their taxes. The denarius, with its imprint of Tiberius, is the symbol of stable currency and commerce for which Romans and provincials could be grateful. If the *pax Romana* and its attendant economic stability were to continue, then Rome needed the appropriate resources. Reminders by Luke and Paul to pay one's taxes were not directed to a Roman official, but to the questioning Christian. Continued debate on this issue could only end in disaster. Christians, according to Luke, would do well to come to terms with their fiscal obligation to the government.

5. Kings and benefactors: Jesus' discourse on ranking (Luke 22: 24–7)

Almost without exception those who comment on Luke 22:24–7 see in Jesus' words sarcasm, irony, criticism, and invective hurled against the rulers of the Roman empire.[116] The statement, they say, reflects Jesus' critical attitude toward the state.[117] Fewer scholars take these verses to be neutral in assessing the empire.[118] Jesus neither condemns nor condones the rulers of the secular realm, but points out that his disciples are to be grounded in a different philosophy of rank and greatness; true greatness consists of service.[119]

Easton rightly asserts that to understand the tone of Luke's statement we need to contrast it with Mark 10:42–5.[120] Indeed, it is this passage from Luke's source that places before us the notion that Jesus is sarcastically comparing those who 'appear to rule over the gentiles' and the one who 'wishes to be great' in the Christian community. Those supposed rulers actually subdue/domineer (κατακυριεύουσιν) and tyrannize (κατεξουσιάζουσιν) their people.[121] The Christian disciple, on the other hand, 'is to be servant of all' (ἔσται πάντων δοῦλος). The contrast is broad and deep, leaving no doubt in the mind of the reader about the differences between secular and Christian ranking and rule.

Luke, however, has carefully adjusted the Marcan vocabulary in order to portray the *imperium* in a favorable light.[122] For him there is no question that the gentile kings, and most assuredly the Roman emperor, reign over the world; they do not merely 'appear to rule.'[123] This rule (κυριεύουσιν) Luke accepts as just and legitimate for he removes the harsh preposition (κατά) from Mark's compound verb.[124] The Marcan word has a sting that Luke eliminates; kings rule their subjects as they ought.

In a similar way Luke removes the sting of Mark's κατεξουσιάζειν. Here Luke is even more positive about the value to secular rule. Not only does he discount the 'tyranny' of the 'great ones,' the Third Evangelist also makes the claim that those who have authority (οἱ ἐξουσιάζοντες) are called 'Benefactors' (εὐεργέται καλοῦνται).

The question has been raised by several commentators as to whether one should take the verb καλοῦνται as a middle or passive voice. Are those in authority given the title 'Benefactor' or do they assume it for themselves? Those who see in this passage sarcasm toward the empire are inclined to regard the verb in the middle sense. It is difficult to believe, however, that Luke does other than reflect the practice of the urban populace who often proclaimed a benefactor as εὐεργέτης.[125] Those who rule in the secular realm are not oppressors of the people, but are in a position to dispense divine benefits to the people. Even though the disciples are to implement a different order of rank, there is no mockery in Luke's use of the title 'Benefactor.' It is both popularly acclaimed and divinely ordained.[126]

6. Conclusion

This review of the political material in Luke—Acts leads one to the inescapable conclusion of C. K. Barrett: 'No Roman official would have filtered out so much of what to him would be theological and ecclesiastical rubbish in order to reach so tiny a grain of relevant apology.'[127] Moreover, there is much in the Lucan material to cast at least a shadow of suspicion on the Christian movement. There is more merit, I believe, in turning the political apologetic around. Luke has presented his reader with a history describing where the church has been in her encounter with the empire; in this account Luke has also helped his reader understand more completely the relationship of the church and state in the ongoing world through a decidedly pro-Roman apologetic.

We turn now to Luke's presentation of the trials of Jesus and Paul[128] which preserve for us a literary treasure of primary information about Roman judicial procedure. More importantly, these trials reveal Luke's own perspective about the relationship between the empire and the church, a perspective that Luke felt compelled to offer his church.

3

THE TRIAL OF JESUS

Near the close of his Gospel, Luke describes the moving story of two disciples conversing with their risen, but veiled and apparently uninformed, master. The disciples say to their fellow-traveler on the road to Emmaus: 'Jesus of Nazareth was a prophet mighty in deed and word ... but our chief priests and rulers handed him over to a judgment of death and they crucified him' (Luke 24:19–20). This statement is the earliest explicit declaration which blames the Jewish leaders for the death of Jesus.[1] A close examination of the trial and death of Jesus in the Third Gospel reveals how sharply Luke has carved the contrast between Jewish and Roman judicial process, subtly shifting the burden of responsibility for Jesus' death from the Romans to the Jews. According to Luke, the Jewish 'trial' was not a trial at all, but the chaotic prelude to an unjust execution which even Roman jurisprudence could not overcome. The will of God, the δεῖ of the Gospel, was to be accomplished in spite of the finest and the worst of human judicial institutions. Four sections of the trial narrative clearly exhibit the Lucan perspective: the Sanhedrin hearing, the Roman trial, Jesus before Herod, and finally the mocking, crucifixion, and ultimate verdict.

A. The Sanhedrin hearing

The shift of responsibility for Jesus' death from the Roman prefect to the Jewish leadership is but one illustration of the way in which Luke has modified his Marcan source to conform with his political perspective. Compared with the Marcan account, Luke offers an unstructured, unordered scene. There is no initial charge which accused Jesus of intending to destroy the temple, no accusing witnesses, no testimony, and not even a formal verdict. While Mark attempts to reconstruct a legitimate Sanhedrin trial, Luke sets out to destroy any semblance of legitimacy. By comparison with the Roman trial which follows, the hearing before the Sanhedrin is a mockery; it is not a trial by Roman standards. Though Luke has followed his source's outline of the trial scene,[2] his additions and omissions bring into sharp relief the difference between Jewish and Roman justice.

In keeping with his conclusion that Jesus did not receive a proper trial before the Sanhedrin, Luke has omitted the search for witnesses against Jesus, which Mark portrays as taking up much of the night (14:55–61a). Luke went straight to the point of the council meeting: to establish a charge against Jesus. The council met at daybreak, put two questions to the accused, and led him off to Pilate. The whole affair, as Luke presents it, need not have taken long.

As Luke describes the events before the council two questions are asked of Jesus, two questions which are really halves of a single Marcan question. Thus, Mark's 'Are you the Christ, the son of the Blessed?' (14: 61) becomes 'If you are the Christ, tell us ...; then, are you the Son of God?' (22:67, 70). In this division Luke has sharpened and clarified the political and religious dimension of the charges which were brought against Jesus. 'Messiah' *must* be distinguished from 'Son of God.' Luke has made clear to his readers that the Sanhedrin knew the *politico-religious* distinction, nevertheless, the council chose, in its accusation to Pilate, to place the emphasis solely on the political side.[3]

Jesus' response to the council reveals that for Luke Jesus' only claim to leadership was a religious one. To the question about messiahship, Jesus gives a most obscure answer, certainly nothing like a confession. 'If I tell you, you will not believe; and if I ask you, you will not answer' (Luke 22: 68). But to the question about divine sonship, Jesus' response is most pointed. If the Sanhedrin wants to present *that* charge in a Roman court, namely that Jesus is the Son of God, then 'you say that I am' (Luke 22:70).

A few commentators have considered Jesus' response simply to be affirmative and rhetorical, a response which is seized by the Sanhedrin as a proof of guilt.[4] Luke's purpose, however, was more qualified;[5] the Third Evangelist wanted his readers to be certain that any charge brought before Pilate should have had *only* a religious content, which he would have – out of ignorance more than anything else – summarily dismissed.[6]

The council concluded its hearing with the question: 'What further need have we of [Jesus'] testimony?' (Luke 22:71). By delicately, but deliberately, altering the Marcan form of this question, Luke has reinforced his anti-Sanhedrin stance. In Mark 14:63 the high priest finished the interrogation of Jesus by asking the council: 'What further need have we of witnesses?' It was Mark's assumption that the Sanhedrin had attempted to establish the case against Jesus by receiving the testimony of at least two witnesses.[7] Having satisfied this legal requirement, the high priest was ready to bring the case to Pilate.

In Luke's hands, however, Mark's 'witnesses' (μαρτύρων), is changed to 'testimony' (μαρτυρίας). Luke has used the singular noun ('testimony') to emphasize that *only* Jesus' testimony was heard and therefore the Sanhedrin violated its own rules of due process.

Luke's account of the Sanhedrin's charges against Jesus is precise and damaging. He has made clear what his source left vague: 'We found this man guilty of perverting our nation, forbidding us to give tribute to Caesar, and claiming that he himself is an anointed one [which means in your language, Pilate], a king!'[8] Pilate's query — 'Are you the king of the Jews?' — also received clarification on the lips of the chief priests. Not three verses after Luke revealed the Sanhedrin's only possible charge against Jesus (i.e., the claim of divine sonship) does the council present precisely the other, political, side of the issue: the man was a Zealot king, inciting the people, teaching them throughout all Judea, from Galilee, the land of the rebels, even to this place.[9]

B. The Roman trial

Jesus, after being charged by the Jewish leaders with treason, was asked by Pontius Pilate: 'Are you the king of the Jews?' Luke following his source, has Jesus reply, Σὺ λέγεις. Then, most remarkably, Pilate pronounces Jesus' innocence: Οὐδὲν εὑρίσκω αἴτιον (23:4). It is incredible that Pilate should have no reservations about a charge of sedition, first, because of his well-known attitude toward rebel suspects, and secondly, because the charge brought against Jesus was presented by the pro-Roman party. Furthermore, Pilate, if he was at all sensible and ambitious, would have wanted to call attention to his prestige (*auctoritas*) by sending a brief of the case of a rebel king to Rome before making a judgment.[10] There is also good reason to believe that Pilate would have been able to remit such a case to the court at Rome if he did not feel competent to dispose of it in Jerusalem.[11] But Pilate, Luke would like to show, could not discover enough evidence, either in the Jewish charges or in Jesus' reply, to proceed with a criminal trial.

It would have been difficult for a Roman citizen familiar with Roman judicial practice — not to mention the twentieth-century historian — to understand Pilate's quick judgment. With such a case of treason, Pilate should have proceeded further with this case *extra ordinem*.[12] A Roman court would not have been content with any other than its own investigation. Pilate's handling of the case, as Luke presents it, renders suspect the theory that Luke is writing an apology to the officials of the empire on behalf of the Christian church. It would have been sheer foolishness for Luke to have intended this trial as a basis for arguing that Pilate's gentle treatment of Jesus ought to suggest to the Roman government an equally favorable stance toward the church. Reading this account, a Roman magistrate would have concluded that Roman justice, as carried out by the prefect, had failed. The trial scene reconstructed by Luke cannot have been intended for Roman magistrates, but was instead given to the church to help it better appreciate the person of the prefect and the 'fairness' — of the imperial judicial system.

Much has already been written in summary form about the mean, cruel, and capricious rule and person of Pilate.[13] Yet, nothing in our primary sources indicates that he grossly undermined Roman justice. That Tiberius left him in office for an extraordinarily long term of ten years attests that he probably represented Roman justice well. Josephus, of course, gives his own biased account of Pilate's dealings with the Jews, yet even the Jewish historian has some difficulty in carrying through a totally bleak picture of the prefect. Pilate does remove the standards from Jerusalem after the Jews bring suit; later, when his soldiers attack to disperse a complaining mob, they do so with far greater vigor than Pilate had commanded — the Jews were not to be killed, only dispersed. If Josephus wrote his accounts of Pilate in the *Jewish War* at approximately the same time as Luke was compiling his Gospel, then it would not be unreasonable to assume that Luke and his readers were familiar with the stories that eventually made up Josephus' picture of Pilate, a picture of special interest to Christians. In the face of the popular Jewish portrait of Pilate, Luke has done his best to show the innocence of both Pilate and the one standing before him.

Luke stands at the beginning of a long line of Christian writers who consciously praise the Romans at the expense of the Jews. Paul Winter states:

> There is a definite connection between two facts; the more
> Christians are persecuted by the Roman state, the more generous
> becomes the depiction of Pontius Pilate as a witness to Jesus'
> innocence. ... The stratagem of depicting Pilate as being unwilling
> to sentence Jesus to death is in line with the general pattern of
> Jewish, and subsequent Christian, apologetics addressed to the
> Roman authorities.[14]

This may be true for writers of the second and third centuries, but it is an unlikely motivation for the Evangelists (and especially for Luke), who were solely concerned to convince the church, not the empire, that Jesus' death was not a travesty of Roman justice, but part of God's plan for salvation.[15]

Even though Pilate had proclaimed Jesus' innocence — indicating to Luke's church that Roman magistrates are just in their judgments — the plan of God could not be overcome even by Roman law. When Bultmann, and almost every other New Testament scholar, says that 'apologetic grounds underlie those features which acquit the Romans and place all responsibility on the Jews,' one must wonder to whom the apologetic is being made.[16]

C. Jesus before Herod

During the initial phase of the trial Pilate learned that Jesus was from Galilee; accordingly, the prefect sent Jesus to the tetrarch of Galilee, Herod Antipas. Of all our first-century sources, this narrative gives us the only instance of direct dealings between Pilate and Herod, though they both held long contemporary reigns. Moreover, the Lucan narrative is so cryptic about this episode that one can do little more than speculate about *why* Pilate sent Jesus to Herod. Scholars have covered the possibilities rather well, advancing five major theories.

First, Pilate may have wanted to rid himself of a difficult and incomprehensible case.[17] In the light of Pilate's personal interest in other cases of suspected rebels, this does not seem likely. If Pilate was seeking Herod's opinion in the matter — after all Herod, the half-Jew, ought to have some understanding of such things as the meaning of 'anointed one' — Herod was of no help; the tetrarch did not even return a brief of the hearing. Pilate can only infer that a decision of innocence was made by the tetrarch for Herod returned the accused.

A second theory suggests that Pilate sought to placate the tetrarch for the massacre which he brought on Galileans visiting Jerusalem.[18] This is possible, though we know virtually nothing about the circumstances attending the event in which Pilate 'mingled [Galilean blood] with their sacrifices' (Luke 13:1). Nor does Pilate, in other instances where Jews, including Galileans, are slaughtered in Jerusalem, show fear of reprisal from (or need of reconciliation with) the tetrarch of Galilee.

Thirdly, it has been speculated that Luke may have had contacts with the house of Herod from which he drew this special information.[19] This is possible, though one is led to ask why Luke neglected the most well-attested story about the tetrarch, the beheading of John the Baptist. Furthermore, the suggestion of a special source does not address the question of why Pilate sent Jesus to Herod.

The fourth possibility is intriguing, but also doubtful. Perhaps Pilate was legally bound to send Jesus to Herod under a law of *forum domicilii.*[20]

In Acts 23:34—5 Felix inquires about Paul's natal home, but he does not send him back to Tarsus for trial — though there is every indication that the procurator could have done just that. According to a decree of Octavian, a Roman citizen could choose to be tried in the court of his native land or free city. That this privilege would have been extended to Jesus, a peasant from Galilee, is hardly likely. Furthermore, Pilate would have waited until Herod returned to his place of rule before transferring Jesus' case to him. A. N. Sherwin-White has suggested that Herod Antipas may have enjoyed his father's extraordinary privilege of extraditing offenders.[21] But it is doubtful that the younger Herod, with his greatly reduced power and only marginal prestige, would have been able to retain this right.

While the above four hypotheses assume that Luke is reporting what he considers to be an historical event, M. Dibelius and H. J. Cadbury suggest that Luke himself worked up the story from Psalm 2:1—2.[22] Thus Luke depicts Herod and Pilate as representatives of the 'kings and rulers' who 'rise up against the Lord and his anointed.' In Acts 4:25—6 Luke has quoted this psalm and stated exegetically that all the powers of the world were arrayed against Jesus, 'both Herod and Pontius Pilate, with the Gentiles and the peoples of Israel' (v. 27). Even though Herod, as Luke certainly knew,[23] was no king, this is a most convincing theory about the genesis of the tradition. However, I believe there is more to the inclusion of the Herod episode than the fulfillment of Psalm 2.

Many scholars have maintained that Luke has structured his presentation of Paul's trial after the trial of Jesus.[24] Thus, as the Third Gospel ends with Jesus' trial, so Acts ends with the trial of Paul; just as Jesus' suffering is foretold by the prophets, so Paul's is predicted by the prophet Agabus (Acts 21:10—14); and the charges against Paul are in many respects similar to those brought against Jesus (Luke 23:2, 5; Acts 17:67; 21: 28; 24:5—6). It might be, however, that Luke has reversed his process in developing the story of Jesus before Herod. Perhaps Luke has styled the account in the Gospel *after* the lavish and full account that he has included in Acts 26. Here Paul gives his last, grand apology before Herod Agrippa, Festus, Bernice, and all the great men of Caesarea. Luke would not allow Jesus to be treated less fairly than his apostle, so he is also made to appear before a Herodian.

Furthermore, Luke has used this scene to portray the mocking of Jesus, thus lifting it away from the Marcan context, Pilate's court. As J. M. Creed remarks, Luke was perhaps 'glad to transfer the outrage from the soldiery of Rome to the soldiery of the local tetrarch.'[25] The half-Jew Herod and his soldiers serve Luke's purpose well. In Luke's scheme, Pilate and Rome are ultimately innocent of Jesus' blood, Herod must bear responsibility for Jesus' shame, and the leaders of the Jews are responsible for his death. Herod, the half-Jewish vassal of Rome, provides the link between the empire and the Sanhedrin.[26]

D. The capital punishment and ultimate verdict

After receiving Jesus back into his custody, Pilate again announces that no specific criminal charge could be sustained against Jesus, nor did Herod find him guilty. Luke adds, 'Therefore after chastising (παιδεύσας) him, I will release him.' Thus in 23:16, as in verse 23, Luke distinguishes the type of beating which Pilate has in mind for Jesus; he tempers the φραγελλώσας suggested by his source (Mark 15:15b) with παιδεύσας.[27] Both Mark and Luke are accurate, at least from their own perspectives, about the type of beating ordered by Pilate. While Luke suggests the lightest form of Roman beating (*fustigatio*), given as a warning to potential trouble-makers, Mark's Latinism (from *flagello*) represents the most severe of Roman whippings which always accompanied a capital sentence. There can be no question that Luke has consciously omitted the Roman pre-crucifixion scourging, a procedure he was informed about by his source (Luke 18:32/Mark 10:34; cf. Mark 15:15b).[28]

With the term παιδεύσας, Luke did more than use 'a light word to express the terrible *flagellatio*,' as A. Plummer suggests.[29] Luke was concerned to show an entirely different perspective from that of his source. For Luke, there never really was a criminal trial. Pilate was prepared to let Jesus go with only a warning, though a firm one, in the form of a lesson by the rod.

Further evidence that Luke did not consider this to have been a completed trial is the curious way he presents the sentencing. Unlike Mark, Luke uses the technical phrase for the passing of a sentence: καὶ Πιλᾶτος ἐπέκρινεν (23:24). Yet the specification of punishment is totally unexpected. Luke has omitted the obvious result and most important aspect of a capital trial — that Jesus was sentenced to scourging and crucifixion (παρέδωκεν τὸν Ἰησοῦν φραγελλώσας ἵνα σταυρωθῇ [Mark 15:15]) — and replaced it with the obscure statement, 'but Jesus he delivered up to their will', (τὸν δὲ Ἰησοῦν παρέδωκεν τῷ θελήματι αὐτῶν [23:25]). Luke did not mention the pre-crucifixion scourging because he did not consider this case to have been a completed Roman trial.[30]

Luke's passion narrative draws to a close with a chain of events linked together by a mysterious third person plural pronoun: *they* led him away; *they* seized one Simon of Cyrene; and when *they* came to a place called 'The Skull,' there *they* crucified him, *they* cast lots to divide his garments. Who, the reader asks, are 'they'? Most naturally we conclude that 'they' were Romans, especially after reading Mark. There are, in fact, two passages in the Lucan crucifixion scene which seem to point to Roman involvement, but the Evangelist has done his best to set that involvement in a light favorable to the empire.

First, in 23:36 Luke states that 'the soldiers also mocked him.' In question, of course, is the identity of the soldiers. That they were Roman is far from certain, Luke having eliminated Mark's reference to the Praetorium. More likely, Luke is implying that the soldiers were either the temple police or Herod's palace guard.[31] Both groups of soldiers have already mocked Jesus.[32] Furthermore, the last named persons to whom 'they' might refer are 'the chief priests and the rulers' (23:13). Luke's ambiguous use of 'they' has allowed him yet another opportunity to implicate Jewish leaders in the crucifixion.

The second reference to soldiery at the cross is Luke's presentation, following Mark, of the Roman centurion and his confession (23:47). While Luke uses ambiguous innuendo to vilify the Jews and their guard, he uses the explicit statement of the centurion to further exculpate the Romans. The Roman soldier provides Luke with the finishing touch for his trial and crucifixion narrative. Instead of having the lone Roman centurion make a confession of faith before the cross (Mark 15:39) — a confession better reserved for Luke's second volume (Acts 10–11) — the centurion gives the final Roman verdict: Ὄντως ὁ ἄνθρωπος οὗτος δίκαιος ἦν: 'This man was truly innocent.'[33]

E. The fall of Jerusalem

Henry Cadbury in his magnificent work *The Making of Luke–Acts,* explores Luke's interest in urban life. The Third Evangelist writes about cities and no city interests him more than Jerusalem. Of the 54 times Jerusalem is mentioned in the synoptics, Luke can claim 60 percent of these occurrences. These references are about evenly divided between Jerusalem as a geographic location and Jerusalem as the subject of Jesus' discourses.[34] Even though, as Conzelmann has made clear, Jerusalem is an important geographical locus for the Third Evangelist, our primary concern is with Jesus' four discourses on the Holy City. In one the resurrected Lord commands the disciples to remain in Jerusalem until they 'are clothed with power from on high.'[35] In the remaining three pericopes — Luke 19:41–4; 21:20–4; 23:28–31 - Jesus foretells the pending doom of the city.[36]

Building on the work of Conzelmann, Helmut Flender discovers that these three passages form a framework upon which the passion story is constructed. The passion narrative begins with Jesus' oracle in 19:41–4 and ends with his warning in 23:27–31. Luke 21:20–4 marks the midpoint (and focus?) of the passion narrative. Two events, the crucifixion of Jesus and the destruction of Jerusalem, are linked in the mind of the Evangelist.[37]

The Lucan writings bear witness to the importance that the city of Jerusalem holds for early Christians. Not only was it the place of Jesus' circumcision and consecration, but the goal of his pilgrimage and place of his death. Jerusalem is where the disciples first see their risen Lord, the mother city for the church, the site of the first Christian council, and the locus of travel for the apostles, especially Paul, through whom the Asian churches gladly send their support for the Jerusalem congregation: 'Gentile Christians might be free from Judaism, but they remained debtors to Zion.'[38]

Luke's church, not yet far removed from its Jewish roots, would have been especially concerned about the loss of the 'center of the world' to the imperial pagans. L. Gaston has examined the eschatological expectation which was tied to the destruction of the Holy City.[39] Once the city had fallen the end of the age would quickly come. Certainly Mark 13 suggests, and Luke 21 reflects, this notion. But whereas the Marcan oracle looks forward to the fall of the city and cosmos, the Third Evangelist had lived through the destruction of Jerusalem and the expected cosmic catastrophe had not come; the end was 'not yet.' A serious question must have confronted Luke: were Christian hopes misplaced? Can the shock waves of the destruction of the center of the world be absorbed by the ongoing history of the empire? Perhaps we can venture into the mind of Luke for an answer. The Christian hope for the end of history attendant upon the fall of Jerusalem was not ill considered, only partially understood. With the destruction of AD 70 the church, at least the Jerusalem branch, was thrown into chaos; the end of history had indeed come for the Jerusalem-dominated church. Yet for the church universal a new beginning was now possible, 'the times of the Gentiles' *were* at hand. The cosmos had not dissolved; the imperial system was not shaken; only the center of gravity had shifted from Jerusalem to Rome.[40] It was now time to proclaim to the church that if it is to survive to the end, it must learn to do so in the context of the imperial political system.

One could read Luke's entire second volume as his answer to the problem of the loss of the Holy City and its Temple. Just as in the Old Testament the 'name,' 'word,' and 'glory' of God rested on the city as signs of

the divine presence, exalting the city to holy status,[41] so, according to
Luke, the primitive Christian community bears the same marks of God's
presence.[42] And just as the destruction of Jerusalem by Nebuchadnezzar
in 586 BC came about only after the divine presence left the city, so now
the 'scattered' (διασπαρέντες) church is to bear the 'name,' 'word,' and
'glory' of God away from Jerusalem 'to the ends of the earth.'[43] 'The
Way' carries not only the witnessing disciples of Jesus, but also the marks
of the divine presence. Jerusalem, stripped of its divine perquisites, may be
profaned by Titus and his Roman troops.

We can make two rather neat stacks out of the recent writings on Jesus'
three oracles about the destruction of Jerusalem. In one stack we find such
scholars as V. Taylor, T. W. Manson, and C. H. Dodd. Their discussions of
Jesus' prophetic oracles primarily focus on Luke's *method*. In the other
stack which bears Germanic names such as Conzelmann, Marxsen, and
Flender, clearly the thrust is to uncover Luke's peculiar *message* to the
church.[44]

It is clear from reading the English literature that Luke has stylized the
oracles of Jesus to fit the Old Testament prophetic pattern. Not only is
Luke attempting to be true to the Palestinian setting of these oracles, as
Cadbury would suggest,[45] but he enhances the prophetic quality of the
sayings of Jesus by having Jesus speak in the Septuagintal [!] language
of the prophets. The oracles of Jesus are given an authentic 'Biblical'
style and the veracity of this prophet is borne out in history. The readers
of Luke's gospel would trace the oracles back, not to Jeremiah, Isaiah, or
Ezekiel, but to Jesus. With a dramatic flair, Luke has presented the
'*ipsissima verba*' of Jesus (translated into Greek of course!) against the Holy
City. Just as Pilate thrice pronounced that the Roman court found Jesus
innocent, so three times Jesus alludes to the court scene of the prophets
and pronounces divine judgement on Jerusalem (Luke 19:41–4; 21:20–4;
23:27–31).

From the German side we are led to see that Luke is concerned to
share with his readers a message about the Holy City. The message is that
the destruction of Jerusalem and the death of Jesus are events that must
be seen in concert. One does not understand the destruction of Jerusalem
apart from the crucifixion. Rome is the chosen instrument of God which,
having once had its own justice thwarted at the trial of Jesus, is thereby
ordained to destroy the city and those institutions that stand in the
way of justice. The destruction of Jerusalem is the logical conclusion
to the passion; the death of Jesus and the fall of the Holy City are jux-
taposed in the compact narratives of Luke 19–23 – from the time Jesus

triumphantly enters Jerusalem until the crowds return home 'beating their breasts.'[46]

At one point, however, we must raise an objection to the German, especially Conzelmann's, understanding of these oracles. According to Conzelmann these prophecies are part of the political apologetic directed to Rome. The destruction of Jerusalem 'is spoken of as punishment';[47] Jerusalem and the Jews were being punished by the Roman army for their 'obstinate superstition' in which 'all that the Jews hold profane' the Romans deemed sacred.[48] A Roman official would not have needed Luke's gospel for that insight. For the Roman there would have been little concern shown over the destruction of Jerusalem, because Rome, not Jerusalem, was the 'eternal city' and 'center of the world.' To a Roman the destruction of Jerusalem had only this significance: it was a major military victory which hastened the reign of the Flavians.[49]

The Lucan method and message are clear: Luke authenticates Jesus' oracles against Jerusalem by presenting them three times in the Biblical-prophetic language a first-century Christian might expect. The oracles make clear to Luke's church that the Roman army is God's own response to the Sanhedrin's injustice. Luke leaves the eschatological question open, for the oracles occur in both eschatological and non-eschatological contexts. By emphasizing the guilt of the Jewish leaders with regard to the fate of their Holy City and excising the reference to 'the abomination of desolation' from the oracle in Chapter 21, Luke has minimized the sacrilegious nature of Titus' intrusion into the Temple. The Christians have only this to understand: that the Roman government has been divinely chosen to act out the prophecies of Jesus; the empire has a significant place in the divine plan for the salvation of the world.

F. Conclusion

If Luke's apologetic was addressed to some Roman official on behalf of the church, then his presentation of the trial of Jesus would only raise more questions than it answers with regard to the relationship of Roman justice and the Christian church. Why was Pilate so superficial in his investigation of the serious charges against a suspected rebel? Jesus was not even 'examined by torture.' If Jesus really was innocent, why did Pilate not insure his protection? Why would Pilate, charged with thoroughly and fairly administering Roman justice, allow this trial to degenerate to the point of an unjust execution?

On the other hand, there is much in the Lucan narrative which commends the Roman government to the Christian community. It could not be denied that Jesus' death was, in the final analysis, allowed by Pontius Pilate. Yet by comparison with the proceedings before the Sanhedrin and Herod, Jesus was dealt with gently and fairly by the Roman magistrate and the official position to the end maintained Jesus' innocence.

There is perhaps a lesson for Luke's church to learn from these events. Even the most sophisticated of human institutions, Roman law and justice, must on occasion succumb to the chaos of unlawful men in order to set in motion the plan of God. Justice can be perverted by sinful men who seek to thwart the plan of God, but God will work through human chaos as well as human order to bring about new life, the resurrection, the new Israel.

Luke has put into the mouth of Jesus three oracles concerning the destruction of Jerusalem. These oracles were constructed by the Third Evangelist from selected Old Testament prophecies which pointed to the destruction of the Holy City by Nebuchadnezzar in 586 BC. Rome, like Babylon of old, is the instrument of God's judgment. But there the Old Testament prophetic model ceases to be useful for Luke. For the Israelite, exile in Babylon was a threat to be feared; for the Christian, this new 'exile' into the empire was an opportunity to universalize the gospel, an opportunity to be welcomed. Rome had provided the impetus and the way into the world.

4

THE TRIAL OF PAUL

In the first chapter of this book we reviewed the Tübingen suggestion that Luke−Acts was an irenic and apologetic work, an interpretation derived particularly from Luke's second volume. The classic Tübingen formulation held that Acts was written to mediate the differences between Jewish Christians (Petrine) and gentile Christians (Pauline). Furthermore, Luke's record of the encounters between Christians and the authorities of the state was intended to prove the harmlessness of Christianity before a questioning Roman government.

Though the Tübingen interpretation, as we have seen, had serious limitations, the balance which the Tübingen scholars attempted to strike is a worthy goal for any contemporary researcher.[1] They built their interpretation on two basic elements that form the nucleus of the last chapters of Acts: Luke has presented Paul as *both* a Pharisee and a Roman. As a diaspora Pharisee, Paul was an effective bridge between the Jerusalem church and the gentile mission churches. As a Roman citizen, Paul was the perfect spokesman to defend Christian political loyalty in a Roman court.

Paul's political *apologia*, however, takes a rather odd turn. Paul's appeal to his Pharisaism and to his Roman citizenship − to the resurrection and to Caesar − results in a rather muddled, if not unconvincing, political apologetic. If Luke's intention was to persuade a magistrate that Christianity is politically benign, he has again been less than effective an advocate. If, however, he was trying to present Rome in a positive light to the Christian reader, he has succeeded. The last chapters of Acts, dramatically written, bring Paul under the jurisdiction and protection of the Roman court. Before exploring this final Roman−Christian encounter we need to say a few words about Luke's presentation of Paul.

A. Luke the Paulinist − the Pauline apology in Acts

The terms ἀπολογοῦμαι/ἀπολογία appear eighteen times in the New Testament − ten times in the writings of Luke, seven times in Acts 22−8.[2]

'Apology' is not only absent from the other gospels, but where the word appears in Luke's gospel the evangelist seems to allude to such events as occur in the later chapters of Acts. In the non-Lucan writings ἀπολογοῦμαι/ ἀπολογία occurs six times in the Pauline letters, once in the Pastorals, and once in First Peter.[3] Since we shall be attempting to demonstrate that in his presentation of Paul's trial Luke has attempted to be a faithful Paulinist, it would be useful to review the six passages where Paul has used the term 'apology.'[4]

Twice in his letters Paul understands his adversaries to be on the defensive. In Rom 2:15 the gentiles' own 'conflicting thoughts' will 'accuse or even defend' (κατηγορούντων ἤ καὶ ἀπολογουμένων) them on the day of judgment. Writing to the Corinthian church, Paul points out that his 'tearful letter' has brought them 'godly grief' which has produced among them 'a repentance that leads to salvation ... [and an] eagerness to clear away the charges [ἀπολογίαν]' (2 Cor. 7:10−11).

In the remaining four Pauline passages, 'apology' is used to indicate the apostle's own defense. Twice Paul defends his apostleship before skeptical Corinthian Christians (1 Cor. 9:3; 2 Cor. 12:19). In both passages the apostle's demeanor, works, and vision of Christ attest to the authority of his calling.

It is only in his letter addressed to the Philippians that Paul uses 'apology' in an unambiguously legal context.[5] One of the important issues for Paul in this epistle is to clarify why he is in prison. To state it quite simply, Paul is in prison 'for a defense of the gospel' (1:7, 16). Even though he is confronted with a serious legal matter which could lead to life or death, he has seized the opportunity to present and to estbalish the truth of the gospel (that Christ has been raised from the dead)[6] among his hearers. While Paul has coupled together the technical courtroom terms ἀπολογία and βέβαιος,[7] there is no hint in this letter of the relevant judicial issues involved in the case nor any mention of the civil or criminal charges which have been brought against the apostle. There are two other items in this letter which deserve to be mentioned. First, Paul lists his credentials: he is of the people of Israel, the tribe of Benjamin, a Hebrew, a Pharisee, a former persecutor of the church, yet in the matter of righteousness, blameless (3:5−6). Secondly , Paul declares that his righteousness transcends law, for it comes from God through faith in Christ, 'that if possible I may attain the resurrection from the dead' (3:9−11).[8]

Luke has skillfully woven thematic threads supplied by Paul into his own tapestry of the apostle's trial: Paul is on trial not to defend himself against any specious charges, but to bear witness to the gospel (Acts 25: 18−19); the heart of that gospel message − that God raises the dead − is a portion of Pharisaic theology that Paul the Pharisee takes seriously (23:6; 26:2–8, 22–3); Paul is righteous (innocent of any wrong doing) before God, and this innocence ought to extend to the human realm where Paul the Roman citizen has transgressed neither Roman nor Jewish law (25:8).

Luke, the faithful Paulinist, has given his readers the drama of Paul's trial, which could well have been drawn from sketches offered by the apostle himself either through his letter to the Philippians,[9] or from a tradition based on that letter, or by direct contact with the situation described in Philippians.[10] In any case, Luke has cast the story in phrases and pictures that truly represented the apostle's own response to his legal situation; the remainder of this chapter is devoted to an examination of that representation.

Conzelmann has placed great emphasis on the Lucan political apologetic. As a key passage by which we may understand the apologetic motif, Conzelmann points to Acts 25:16. In that verse the Roman procurator Festus tells King Agrippa, 'it is not the custom of the Romans to hand over any one before the accused has met his accusers face to face, and had opportunity to make a defense ($\dot{\alpha}\pi o\lambda o\gamma\dot{\iota}\alpha\varsigma$) concerning the charges leveled against him.' This passage, Conzelmann claims, underlines the legal position of Paul and the protection afforded him by the judicial processes of the empire. 'Significantly there is no mention of the relation to Judaism, and reference is made only to the Roman procedure. The problem is not that of the relationship between Christianity and Judaism ..., but of [Paul's] civil rights.'[11]

Though Conzelmann is correct in stressing that in Acts there is no attempt to prove that Christianity is a *religio licita*,[12] he does the Lucan Paul a disservice and misunderstands Luke the Paulinist by claiming that 'in connection with the State *only* political and legal arguments are used.'[13] As we shall see, that simply is not true; Luke does not so neatly divorce 'religious apologetic' from 'political apologetic' in the trial of Paul. Rather, political and religious issues are always interwoven in Paul's legal defense.[14] Even though the Pauline 'religious apologetic' might confuse a Roman magistrate, its subtlety would not escape the Christian reader.

B. Paul on trial

It is now our task to uncover, with some precision, the charges against Paul, the nature of the defense that the Lucan Paul develops with respect to the charges, and how this defense corresponds to Luke's pro-Roman political perspective. There are four hearings in which Paul is called on to make an apology: before 'the men of Israel' and Claudius Lysias (Acts 21:

27 − 23:30), Felix (24:1−27), Festus and his council (25:6−12), and
Festus and Agrippa (25:13 − 26:32).[15]

1. Paul before 'the men of Israel' and Lysias[16]

In Acts 21:28 the first accusations are made by certain 'Jews from Asia.'
Paul stands accused of 'teaching men everywhere against the people
and the law and this place, moreover he also brought Greeks into the
Temple and defiled this holy place.' The accusation was made not to
the Roman court but to the 'men of Israel' in Jerusalem. Claudius Lysias,
the Roman tribune, quickly arrested Paul, thereby rescuing him from
the hands of an angry mob. It was the maintenance of Roman order,
and not necessarily interest in the Jewish charges, that compelled the
tribune to act.

Luke indicates that Lysias made an attempt to ascertain the charges
against Paul. If Paul was indeed a teacher 'who introduces new religious
doctrines ... by which the minds of men are influenced,'[17] then he might
have been culpable under Roman law. But Luke consistently paints
a picture of Paul in colors distinctly Jewish. Paul was the representative
of the Christian sect of Judaism, a sect having much in common with the
Pharisees. Paul ends this particular discussion with a reminder that he is
(present tense) a Pharisee; the resurrection is no 'new religious doctrine.'

The second charge against Paul is the more serious. Josephus reports
that the Jews engraved a clear warning in Greek and Latin on the balus-
trade of the Temple which forbade the entrance of foreigners into the
holy place.[18] If we are to believe Josephus, the capital punishment resulting from an infraction of this prohibition extended even to Roman citizens.
Luke does suggest that the Jews tried to kill Paul outside the Temple
and that Rome intervened to rescue him. Of course it is not at all certain
that capital punishment extended to one who brought foreigners into
the Temple, as well as the foreigner himself.[19] Neither is it certain that
Paul did in fact bring a non-Jew into the Temple for Luke reports that
the Asian Jews had only seen Trophimus in Jerusalem with Paul. When
they later found the apostle in the Temple, the unsound deduction was
made that the Greek had followed Paul into the place of worship.[20]

We observed in Luke's presentation of the trial of Jesus a contrast
between well ordered Roman justice and chaotic Jewish legal practice.
The same stereotypes are present in the trial of Paul. The Asian Jews
and the amorphous irrational mob are set in radical contrast to the
reasoned, orderly approach of Lysias and the Roman cohort. If the
Jews had a law by which Paul could have been capitally sentenced, they

had no orderly means of reaching a verdict. Aside from Roman procedure, the accused had little chance for a defense before his accuser.

The Jewish leaders concluded from this first encounter that Lysias was unlikely to accept a case against the defendant on the charge of 'teaching.' The teaching of the apostle was, in fact, well regarded by the Pharisees who did not disown him. Paul concluded his first defense with an appeal to the orthodox teaching of the Pharisees: 'Brethren, I am a Pharisee, a son of Pharisees; *with respect to the hope and the resurrection of the dead I am on trial*' (Acts 23:6).

2. Paul before Felix

Luke has stitched the first two trial scenes together with a promise and a threat. It is the will of God ($\delta\epsilon\hat{\iota}$), spoken to Paul, that he go to Rome (23:11). The divine will is shortly thereafter threatened by an ambush planned by Paul's adversaries. Once again, Luke has taken occasion to contrast the inadequacy of Jewish 'justice' and the careful protection of the Roman order. The ambush is thwarted and Paul is delivered safely to the court of Felix.

In the second trial scene the cause of the Asian Jews is taken up by the chief-priests and the Sanhedrin. The Jewish leaders, aware that the original charges against Paul were not viable, have their spokesman, Tertullus, present a revised list:

> We found this man
> (1) a pestilent person,[21]
> (2) fomenting rebellion among all the Jews of the empire,[22]
> (3) a ringleader of the sect of the Nazarenes,
> (4) even attempting to profane the Temple.

So in the second trial scene two important changes were made: a charge of treason was added[23] and the original charge of bringing Greeks into the Temple was broadened to facilitate the procurator's understanding and to gain a Roman conviction: Paul had *profaned* the Temple. Luke presented the subtle shift of the latter charge in two ways: (1) the Asian Jews had accused Paul of a *fait accompli* ($\kappa\epsilon\kappa o \acute{\iota}\nu\omega\kappa\epsilon\nu$) while the Sanhedrin, aware of the weak circumstantial evidence, spoke only of Paul's intention ($\dot{\epsilon}\pi\epsilon\acute{\iota}\rho\alpha\sigma\epsilon\nu$ $\beta\epsilon\beta\eta\lambda\tilde{\omega}\sigma\alpha\iota$).[24] (2) The word $\kappa o\iota\nu o\tilde{\upsilon}\nu$ would have strong meaning for a Jew that it would not possess for a Roman; therefore, Luke had the Sanhedrin use another word, $\beta\epsilon\beta\eta\lambda o\tilde{\upsilon}\nu$, a 'secular word' intended for the gentile mind.[25]

The first and third charges against Paul were not serious. Being called 'a perfect pest,' as Moffatt delightfully translates, or 'ring-leader' of a Jewish sect was no crime, unless, of course, that sect was seditious. The second and fourth charges were the more serious and had to be dealt with carefully; if conviction resulted, punishment was severe.

In an excellent survey of the wide range of laws dealing with treason, E. F. Scott states that the laws forbidding *laesa maiestas* were

> applied indiscriminately to every grave offense tending to disturb public peace, the destruction of public order by means of sedition, or the interference with the discharge of their functions by any official of the government and the betrayal of the interests of the State in general, and the impairment of national sovereignty, rather than attacks made directly against the ruler in person as the representative of magisterial and popular power. This doctrine subsequently extended to include all disparaging or insulting remarks aimed at the sovereign or at his subordinates ...[26]

Certainly 'offending against Caesar' and being an 'agitator among the Jews of the empire' falls under the code as *crimen laesae maiestatis*.

With regard to rebellion Paulus writes that 'the authors of a sedition or tumult, or those who stir up the people ... will be deported to an island.'[27] A harsher penalty, death, was meted out to 'those who ... pollute a shrine or temple.'[28] These penalties were specified for those of superior rank (*honestiores*), Paul's rank as a Roman citizen by birth.[29]

In his defense before Felix, Paul says that he neither 'disputed (διαλεγόμενον) with anyone nor stirred up (ἐπίστασιν ποιοῦντα) a crowd in the Temple, in the synagogues, or in the city' (24:12). Paul is most emphatic that the Jews cannot prove this new charge of treason.[30] And to the other serious charge Paul responds that he did not profane the Temple. On the contrary, he was found 'purified (ἡγνισμένον) in the Temple.'[31] Once again Paul concludes his apology by referring to the resurrection: 'It is *with respect to the resurrection of the dead that I am on trial*' (24:21).

3. Paul before Festus and his council

Again, Luke has stitched two trial scenes together with a dramatic narrative of promise and threat. Paul's discussion with Felix raises the level of suspense for the reader. Felix not only has 'rather accurate knowledge of the Way,' he also encourages Paul to provide him with more details about faith in Jesus. The Lucan Paul, however, gives an interesting twist to the discussion. Rather than offering the pious discourse one might expect,

Paul lectures Felix about the high virtues endemic to good Roman magistracy. With Senecan echoes, Paul calls Felix to be just in judgment, to exercise self-restraint, and to remember that he himself must some day be judged.[32]

Felix does not set Paul free, which increases the suspense of this narrative another notch. Moreover, he expected a bribe, and receiving none he left Paul in prison as a favor to the Jews. Such details, unfavorable to Felix, are honest depictions of provincial life. In no way has Luke presented the imperial system of justice as broken. In fact, Luke's description of Felix is far less acrimonious than Tacitus' remark that 'with all manner of cruelty and lust he exercised the power of a king with the mind of a slave.'[33]

The caprice of Felix, however, is overshadowed by the explicit villainy of the Jewish leaders who still hope to ambush and murder Paul. This time Felix's successor, Festus, protects Paul, insisting on the full measure of Roman justice and, at the same time, insuring that Paul and his gospel will reach Rome.

At the third hearing Paul himself does what his prosecutors so far have failed to do; he succinctly and explicitly lays out all the possible charges against him. The apostle, of course, pleads innocent to each. He has violated neither the law of the Jews (with regard to bringing Greeks into the Temple), nor the Temple itself (with regard to Roman prohibitions about temple desecration), nor Caesar (with regard to civil strife).[34] Paul concludes his short defense with an appeal to Caesar. Haenchen quite rightly points out the incomprehensibility of this appeal. Festus has rendered no verdict, Paul does not insist on a continuation of the trial, and Festus himself does not suggest continuing the trial or remitting it to Rome. Haenchen then reminds us that this is not a court transcript, but 'a suspense-laden narrative created by the author.'[35] The procedural inconsistencies are Lucan and they are designed to show how Paul was brought safely to Rome. He is now officially, according to Luke, under imperial security (25:21).

From the Roman point of view, which Luke presents through the statement of Festus to Agrippa, Paul has made his case. The argument between Paul and his accusers involved neither desecration of a temple nor treason, but 'certain points of dispute ... about *their own religion*,' namely, as Paul has twice made clear, 'about one Jesus, who was dead, but whom Paul asserted to be alive' (25:19). Now that Festus and the Roman government understand the nature of the Sadducaic—Christian controversy and the basis of Paul's defense, Luke is ready to move toward the grand finale.

4. Paul before Festus and Agrippa

Luke presents the final courtroom scene in word pictures intended to impress the reader. This is the last hearing accorded Paul in Acts and the grandness of this finale is a prelude of events to come in Rome.[36] Festus the magistrate, Agrippa the king, and Bernice the king's wife 'came together with great pomp, and they entered the audience hall with the military tribunes and the prominent men of the city. Then by command of Festus Paul was brought in' (25:23). As in the trial of Jesus, Luke has stylized the Herodian as a half-way figure. Being neither fully Jewish nor fully Roman, Agrippa has been asked to shed some light on the Jewish charges.[37]

Paul, having gained permission to speak, stretches out his hand in fine rhetorical style and begins his *apologia* with a *captatio benevolentiae*. The reader is now thoroughly impressed by the setting and anxiously awaits the final word from the apostle. If it is a political defense which the reader expects, he will be sorely disappointed, for Paul says nothing of the political charges against him nor does he mention his civil rights. The content of Paul's defense is quite unexpected and, if the charges are political, totally irrelevant. Paul tells of his background as a Jew of the strictest sect who once opposed the Christian movement. He relates his experience on the Damascus road and his call by the risen Christ to become involved in the gentile Christian mission, a mission soundly based on Torah and the prophets. Once again *the apostle closes his defense with a statement about the resurrection.* It is nothing short of amazing that at this last hearing Paul neglects the serious political charges against him. The apology here, as elsewhere, rests almost solely on religious issues.

As in the trial of Jesus, three times the Roman magistrates declared that a case could not be made against the apostle.[38] Moreover, there are two additional passages in which Luke attempts to show that according to Roman standards Paul's case was not serious. After Paul presented his final apology Festus exclaimed that the apostle was mad (Μαίνῃ, Παῦλε); the great learning of this Jew has driven him mad (26:24). If Modestinus' legal opinion is based on courtroom history, then it may be that by pronouncing Paul mad, Festus has acquitted him:

> ... the personal character of the accused should be taken into account, whether he could have committed the offense [of *maiestas*], as well as whether he had previously done or planned anything of the same nature, and also if he was of sane mind (*sanae mentis*) ..., for although the rash person ought to be punished, still they should be excused just as insane (*insanis*) persons are ... (*Dig.* 48.4.7)

The other more frequently cited passage is Agrippa's statement to Festus: 'This man could have been set free if he had not appealed to Caesar.'[39]

5. Conclusion

We must ask again whether Luke intended a Roman official to ascertain from his account of Paul's trial, with all its peculiar theological nuances, an apologetic on behalf of the church (or of Paul)? I think not. The content of Paul's apology, the resurrection, is accurately Pauline.[40] Luke has rightly reported Paul's message, but forced it into a courtroom context that makes little sense. The Christian reader, in fact, may be as confused about this as any Roman magistrate. The importance of these scenes lies not in the details of their forced construction, but in the all-encompassing will of God which uses the Roman court to its own ends. In the Third Gospel, it is the will of God that Jesus be crucified, Roman law notwithstanding; in Acts, divine necessity brings Paul and the gospel to Rome under the aegis of Roman law.[41]

From beginning to end, Luke has designed his work to aid the Christian community in its understanding of the workings of the empire so that the church may begin to develop a dialogue with the local magistrates. Christians, like Paul, need not feel intimidated by untrue accusations nor anxious about being dealt with fairly.

Christianity as a *religio licita* was simply not a matter of consideration for Luke.[42] Moreover, it is doubtful that Luke presented Paul defending his civil rights; Paul everywhere assumes them.[43] The civil rights of the empire not only protect Paul, but are, for Luke, a part of the 'divine necessity' ($\delta\epsilon\hat{\iota}$) by which the gospel (through the person of Paul) reaches the center of the empire, Rome. It is divinely guided Roman law that insures the continuation and growth of the gospel.

Paul's appeal to Caesar was more than a legal action; it was, according to Luke, part and parcel of the divine workings of God in history. Conzelmann concludes his section on Luke's apologetic with these important words. 'In the end it is confidence in the justice of the Emperor that forms the great climax of the narrative. There is no suggestion whatever of any weakening of this confidence.'[44] Nor *should* there be any 'weakening,' for it is God who stands behind those human processes which in the past protected Paul and now, in Luke's day, assist the church in her mission.

C. 'And so we came to Rome'

With these words Luke concludes the odyssey of the Christian gospel from its humble beginnings in a strange and distant land to the very center of the civilized world. One of the striking features of Luke's literature is his ability to expand gently, but steadily, the scope of his narrative. Biography (Third Gospel) becomes history (Acts of the Apostles), a provincial sect grows into a world-wide mission, and the particularistic message of Jesus and the Jerusalem Jewish-Christians develops into the universalistic Pauline message of salvation for the gentiles.[45] Luke closes his two volumes with Paul brought to Rome by means of Roman judicial process and under the protection of the imperial army.[46] In the end, he is able to proclaim openly and freely the Christian message in that great city.[47]

The fair and just legal system of the empire, only hinted at in Jesus's trial, was clearly presented in the trials of Paul. Time and again when Paul and his companions were brought to the authorities for disciplinary action they were protected by the process of Roman law.[48] Even when due process was neglected, as in Thessalonica, the magistrates quickly remedied the situation when challenged by Paul.[49]

But the Roman legal system attempted to be more than just. Its ultimate aim was to provide protection for the populace, especially Roman citizens, against members of the society who would take advantage of others by fraudulent means. Moreover, there were safeguards instituted to protect the individual from the power of the state, especially important when that power was exercised by a malicious or incompetent magistrate.

Throughout the last half of Acts Paul was protected by the imperial courts from false and misleading accusations made by angry Jews and pagans. At the last of his trials, Paul's protection lies in the person of the emperor:

> I stand before Caesar's tribunal, where I ought to be tried; to the Jews I have done no wrong, as you know very well. If then I am a wrong doer, and have committed anything for which I deserve to die, I do not seek to escape death; but if there is nothing in their charges against me, no one can give me up to them. I appeal to Caesar. (Acts 25:10–11)

Even though to Caesar he was sent, the protection of Rome did not end with the appeal but tenaciously continued through the stormy Mediterranean waters. Here the Roman army, in particular its officers, becomes the focus of Luke's presentation. The sea voyage from Caesarea to Rome seems important to Luke and we must ask why the Evangelist devotes so much space to Paul's last journey.

Several commentators point to the last two chapters of Acts as an example of Luke's literary skill. Before Paul is allowed to reach his Roman destiny he must first pass through the penultimate perils of an odyssey. Though it may be debated whether Luke used first person pronouns to heighten the exciting effect of his imaginatively constructed account[50] or whether he is actually reporting his own eye-witness account,[51] it is clear that Lucan scholars have seen little of theological interest in the voyage narrative. In fact, the very incident that looks most theological – the sharing of bread on board ship – is either glossed over as insignificant[52] or dismissed as absurd[53] (we shall return to this point below). Traditional scholarship has concluded that Luke's singular goal was to give his reader an exciting, detailed, and picturesque travelogue.

When the final journey of Paul is reduced to a travel narrative then the researcher is content to investigate the details – nautical terms and practice, ports of call, ancient meteorology, Rome's merchant marine – as, in 1880, did James Smith, whom almost all contemporary scholars repeat with a few additions or corrections.[54] But Luke did not devote such a sizeable portion of material to the journey of Paul from Caesarea to Rome just to give his readers a travelogue. The odyssey of Paul and the Christian message to Rome is the great climax of Luke's apologetic statement. Luke has presented the imperial army working in concert with Roman law and the providence of God to insure the preservation and expansion of the gospel message.

In the midst of the stormy sea, 'when no small tempest lay on us, [and] all hope of our being saved was at last abandoned,' Paul reported the visit of an angel who said, 'Do not be afraid, Paul; you must stand before Caesar; and lo, God has granted you all those who sail with you.' The next dawn Paul promised salvation ($\sigma\omega\tau\eta\rho\iota\alpha\varsigma$) to the crew if they would share a meal with him. Then, 'he took bread, and giving thanks to God ... he broke it and began to eat. Then they were all encouraged and ate some food themselves.'[55]

It is neither by accident nor unconscious habit that Luke combines the giving of thanks to God, the breaking of bread aboard a doomed ship, and the promise of salvation to the ship's passengers. It has been suggested that Acts 27:34–6 is, if not eucharistic,[56] a 'prefiguration' of the eucharist.[57] The words $\tau\sigma\tilde{\upsilon}\tau\sigma\ \gamma\grave{\alpha}\rho\ \pi\rho\grave{\sigma}\varsigma\ \tau\tilde{\eta}\varsigma\ \dot{\upsilon}\mu\epsilon\tau\acute{\epsilon}\rho\alpha\varsigma\ \sigma\omega\tau\eta\rho\acute{\iota}\alpha\varsigma\ \dot{\upsilon}\pi\acute{\alpha}\rho\chi\epsilon\iota$ and $\lambda\alpha\beta\grave{\omega}\nu\ \ddot{\alpha}\rho\tau\sigma\nu\ \epsilon\dot{\upsilon}\chi\alpha\rho\acute{\iota}\sigma\tau\eta\sigma\epsilon\nu\ \tau\tilde{\omega}\ \theta\epsilon\tilde{\omega}\ \dot{\epsilon}\nu\dot{\omega}\pi\iota\sigma\nu\ \pi\acute{\alpha}\nu\tau\omega\nu\ \kappa\alpha\grave{\iota}\ \kappa\lambda\acute{\alpha}\sigma\alpha\varsigma\ \dot{\eta}\rho\xi\alpha\tau\sigma\ \dot{\epsilon}\sigma\theta\acute{\iota}\epsilon\omega$ certainly reflect eucharistic language.

However, five major objections have been raised against such an interpretation of this passage. First, there is no cup mentioned; Paul only 'breaks bread,' a common formula for eating an ordinary meal. Secondly, it was not unusual for Jews to render thanks before meals.[58] Thirdly, 'salvation' has no cosmic connotations here; Luke uses the term in the same sense as he did in Acts 3 and 4 (the healing ['saving'] of the lame man); only life and limb can be saved.[59] Fourthly, would Paul have shared a eucharistic meal with those outside the Christian community?[60] Finally, no words of institution are used. Yet, none of these arguments singly or together destroy the possibility that Luke is conveying to his readers a eucharistic scene.

First, even though we cannot fully trace the early development of eucharistic formula and practice here, we do know that it remained in a state of flux during the first Christian century. Luke's own account of the Lord's supper is considerably different from that presented in the other synoptics.[61] Certainly if wine was unavailable on a half-wrecked ship, it is not inconceivable that the eucharist would have been carried out with bread alone. We should also note that in Luke 24:30 the risen Christ is made known to the disciples in the 'breaking of bread' and in Acts 20:7 Luke uses the 'breaking of bread' (κλάσαι ἄρτον) as the technical term for a eucharist.

Secondly, any attempt by Paul in this scene to relate the breaking of bread to the body of Christ would have been nonsense to the pagans around him. They were interested in salvation from destruction. Presumably the Christian author of the 'we material' and Aristarchus were with Paul during the meal so that at least the three could break bread together and share a eucharist; what more appropriate time? The meal could also have been offered to the others on board ship and presented as 'a meal for your salvation' – not a bad extension of eucharistic theology.[62] But does the saving of life and limb have anything to do with the Lord's supper? It is clear that the early church had already made such a connection. Paul claimed that those who abuse the Lord's supper risk bodily ills and death.[63] The converse, that the eucharist offers the promise of physical salvation, may also have been claimed by the apostle.

Lastly, we note that there is little that is 'unconscious' about this scene. Luke has quite deliberately presented Paul taking the initiative in gathering the crew, soldiers, and prisoners for a meal in the most unlikely place of all in Acts, in the midst of a disastrous storm. A better place for the thanksgiving supper might have been after they reached the safety of land. But it is in the midst of chaos – such theological themes as darkness and the depths of the sea would not be wasted on the reader – that Paul brings the word and the meal of salvation.[64] Paul has promised salvation through the meal which he blesses; Luke's first-century Christian reader would not have glossed this over, nor should we.

The centurion, Julius, also has a part to play in the saving activity of God.[65] He, too, was guided by a commission: to bring Paul safely to Rome. It may be that Julius went well beyond the requirements of his commission. Once the ship had run aground the soldiers were quite correct in wanting to kill the prisoners, since they were accountable with their lives for them.[66] The centurion, however, overruled the request of his men, unshackled the prisoners, and ordered them to swim for safety. Paul was 'saved' by Julius; the gospel was rescued by Rome.[67]

Paul and Julius worked together in fulfilling their mutual salvation, but also for the preservation of the gospel message and imperial justice. The Christian community, especially the community of Rome, may rejoice that God has worked out his purposes and extended the gospel to them by means of the imperial order.

D. Conclusion

We have discovered that Luke, in his attempt to be the faithful Paulinist, has presented Paul in a Roman court denying the criminal charges brought against him by appealing to the resurrection. Such a defense supplied the Christian community with an historical account which augmented Paul's letter to the Philippians. With this account Luke would have his readers understand that all who preceded them in the faith – apostles, teachers, prophets – were blameless before the laws of Judaism and the empire. Christian disputes with Judaism are internal theological matters beyond the comprehension of Roman courts. Luke's reconstruction of Paul's defense reflects the essence of Paul's own political stance: 'Let every person be subject to the governing authorities ... for [they] are ministers of God' (Rom. 13:1–6). There is in Paul no political quarrel with Rome; there is, however, a desire to declare that his detention by Rome has served 'to advance the gospel' (Phil. 1:12). Luke has elaborated on this positive aspect of Paul's hearings; time and again Paul appeals to the resurrection of Jesus as the reason for his arrest and the substance of his defense.

Moreover, we hear in Luke's trial scenes an echo of Josephus' surprising statement, 'Fate (Tύχη) has gone over to the Romans' (*JW* 3.354). The goal of Luke's two volumes, from beginning to end, is Rome. While one can look back with nostalgia on the days of the disciples meeting in the Temple, the call of Luke is to turn one's thoughts from the past to the present.[68] Rome, her politics and policies, is the wave of the present and future. The church would do well to come to terms with the empire.

Even the ending of Acts, which seems so surprisingly abrupt, is consistent with Luke's pro-Roman point of view. In the introductory chapter we noted Schrader's observation that Luke did not include the death of Paul at the hands of Nero because he wanted to maximize the impression that Christianity was an innocent religion. I would rather suggest that Luke suppressed this information (if true) to maintain his positive perspective on the imperial government.[69] Luke therefore closed his writing with Paul free to speak openly in Rome about 'the kingdom of God and ... the Lord Jesus Christ,' subjects not without political nuances. Rome is not only just and powerful; Rome can abide the Christian message.

5

CONCLUDING REMARKS ON THE POLITICAL PERSPECTIVE OF ST LUKE

This investigation of Luke—Acts has led us to turn 'upside-down' (borrowing a phrase from Acts 17:6) the traditional interpretation of Luke's political apologetic. Far from supporting the view that Luke was defending the church to a Roman magistrate, the evidence points us in the other direction. Throughout his writings Luke has carefully, consistently, and consciously presented an *apologia pro imperio* to his church. Where he found anti-Roman innuendos in his sources he has done his best to neutralize such material and to emphasize the positive aspects of Roman involvement in the history of the church. Like Philo and Josephus, Luke has seen governmental intervention in the affairs of his religion, and yet he continues to affirm that the positive benefits of the empire far outweigh the occasional intrusiveness of an errant emperor.[1]

A final question naturally comes to mind. John's apocalypse, Clement's letter, and Tacitus' history suggest that the first-century church had suffered the pangs of state-supported persecution. Would Luke, writing in such an oppressive context, have held a positive view of the empire? This question implies, with Conzelmann, that '*ecclesia pressa*' is an apt description of Luke's 'time of the Church.'[2] According to Conzelmann, this time, in which the church looks back to the earthly ministry of Jesus and forward to the parousia, is a time of political persecution. Yet it is practically impossible to know with certainty the nature of the political relationship between church and state during Luke's time. We can be sure, however, that Conzelmann's description of an oppressed church is not supported by what we know of Rome under the Flavians.

If we assume the *terminus a quo* and the *terminus ad quem* normally ascribed to Luke—Acts, AD 70—90, we note that this was a period of relative tranquillity and tolerance throughout the empire.[3] The enlightened reign of the Flavians — Vespasian and his sons Titus and Domitian — has been well documented.[4] Vespasian (69—79) restored peace, order, and prosperity after the civil war of 69. Titus continued his father's policy of toleration and liberality. Even the first dozen years (81—92) of Domitian's

64

rule went well for the populace. His administration was honest and just; he continued the economic and social policies of his predecessors by which Rome prospered. The emperor and his administration were trusted and respected until the early nineties.[5]

If Luke was at all in touch with the spirit of the times then he would have been optimistic about the future of the church on earth, an optimism revealed throughout the Acts of the Apostles: 'So the church throughout Judea and Galilee and Samaria had peace and was built up; and walking in the fear of the Lord and in the comfort of the Holy Spirit it was multiplied' (Acts 9:31). Even in Rome Paul was able to preach the Kingdom of God and to teach about Jesus 'quite openly and unhindered' (Acts 28:31).

This positive view of the empire must have raised some very complex and difficult problems for Luke. First, we know that some, perhaps much, of the Christian community did not share Luke's perspective. There was a tendency for some to deprecate the imperial government. A speedy and catastrophic end of the empire was anticipated; the kingdom of Caesar would be replaced by the kingdom of Christ. At best, the government could be tolerated until the parousia; at worst, Rome was a ravenous beast.[6] Luke may have been concerned to counter such anti-Roman sentiment in order to help the church survive in the given political order. He reflects Paul's teaching on obedience to the state,[7] and he shares the spirit of Clement's prayer: '... grant that we may be obedient to thy almighty and glorious name, and to our rulers and governors upon the earth. Thou, Master, hast given the power of sovereignty to them through thy excellent and inexpressible might, that we may know the glory and honor given them by thee, and be subject to them, in nothing resisting thy will' (1 Clem. 60.4–61.1).

Secondly, the delay of the parousia weighed heavily on an anxious church whose members were growing old and dying.[8] The delay must have fueled speculation about the nature of the end, increased skepticism about the truth of the Christian message, and raised anxieties about living a circumspect Christian life. Perhaps it was that Luke addressed himself to that element of the church which anxiously awaited the coming of the Lord and saw little value in developing a dialogue with the enduring state.[9] Jesus may indeed be taking longer to return than some would like, but Christians should know that meanwhile God has granted men the earthly tools of law, commerce, and protection which can aid the church in its missionary endeavor to preach the good news to every nation.

The third problem confronting Luke would have been the recent and crushing defeat of the Jewish nation and the consequent severing of the Christian sect from its parent religion. The struggling infant was left to work out its new social relationships with the wider culture without the legal benefits granted Judaism.[10] Judaism had often experienced a difficult time with the process of accommodation; the church would not find the road any easier now that it lacked the legal status of the synagogue. Moreover, following the defeat in Palestine there may well have been some attempts to ascribe blame. Could the new faith be linked with the parties responsible for the Jewish disaster? Did anti-Roman sentiments still smolder in the hearts of the Messianists? Could a group that preached loyalty to 'another king, Jesus,' be trusted? Luke not only defended the Roman government, but he also pointed out how the church may defend itself if an occasion for defense should arise. Paul was able to defend himself by appeal to the resurrection and Roman law; other Christians could do the same.

Finally, Luke did not hesitate to incorporate such notions as 'power' and 'authority' into his writings. Though there are two spheres — church and state — where power and authority are operative in the world, ultimately it is God, the singular source of all power and authority, who controls the political destiny of nations and the religious life of his chosen people. God imparts to the emperor political authority over men which is delegated even to the lowly centurion. Likewise, Jesus has been given spiritual authority which is delegated to the 'least of the apostles.' The state is ordained by God to use its power for the benefit of all by obtaining peace and maintaining harmony among the diverse nations of the world.[11] Likewise, the church is under holy orders to use its δύναμις for the salvation of the human race. With this common source of power and authority and a common objective for humanity, the church could stand in partnership with the empire.

But Luke did more than meet anti-Roman sentiment, anxiety over a delayed parousia, misrepresentation of Christian loyalties, and a potential conflict over the notion of power and authority. Luke was a theologian who, like his contemporaries, could not divorce theology from history. If God was truly at work in the world, then he did his work not only through the church but through the secular realm as well. God has called both church and state into his service. The state may be ignorant of his dual ordination, but the church must not be. Therefore, Luke makes certain that the church is fully cognizant of the divine calling given to both institutions. The empire which has exonerated Jesus and saved Paul can continue to sustain the work of the church through its public administration and services, legal apparatus and protection.

Luke was indeed a theologian, and a theologian who deserves a special place of honor in the canon of saints more because of his practicality than his erudition. At the beginning of this book we pointed out the general agreement among New Testament scholars that Luke was writing from a defensive posture. According to this consensus, he was defending his church against charges of disloyalty, impending persecution, and questions concerning the church's status as a *religio licita*. I hope that at the very least this work has raised the possibility that Luke had another political concern — that he held a positive view of the empire which was shared by several of his literary contemporaries and which he imparted to his reading public. Luke was less concerned about the political stance of the church than he was to defend the imperial government to the church. This aspect of his writing would salve the wounded spirits of those who painfully awaited the parousia and would insure the survival of the church. It is with respect to survival that Luke was a clear-headed, practical theologian *sans égal*. With great skill he was able to blunt the apocalyptic appeal of the anti-Roman wing of the church which he wisely saw as the primary internal threat to the Christian movement.[12] Concurrently he confronted the external threat of rumor, innuendo, and accusation and helped the church to meet this menace.

Luke was a theologian who artistically wove together the component threads of theology — history (tradition), apology (the present situation), and eschatology (hope). Imbedded in his historical narrative was a clear message to the church, an *apologia pro imperio*, which would help the Christian community live effectively with the social, political, and religious realities of the present situation until the advent of God's reign.

NOTES

Preface

1 Cited by W. Gasque, *A History of the Criticism of the Acts of the Apostles* (Tübingen: Mohr, 1975) 21–2; C. A. Heumann, 'Dissertatio de Theophilo, cui Lucas historiam sacram inscripsit,' *Bibliotheca Historico-Philologico-Theologica*, Class. IV (1721) 483–505.
2 W. C. van Unnik, 'Luke–Acts, A Storm Center in Contemporary Scholarship,' *Studies in Luke–Acts*, ed. by L. Keck and J. L. Martyn (Nashville: Abingdon, 1966; hereafter designated *SLA*) 15–32; C. Talbert, 'Shifting Sands: The Recent Study of the Gospel of Luke,' *Interpretation* xxx (1976) 381–95.
3 E. Franklin, *Christ the Lord: A Study in the Purpose and Theology of Luke– Acts* (Philadelphia: Fortress, 1975), represents the former viewpoint; R. Cassidy, *Jesus, Politics, and Society* (Maryknoll, NY: Orbis, 1978) presents the latter.

1. Introduction

1 M. Dibelius, *Studies in the Acts of the Apostles*, tr. by Mary Ling and Paul Schubert (New York: Scribner's, 1956) 133.
2 Cf. R. Bultmann, *History of the Synoptic Tradition*, tr. by John Marsh (New York: Harper and Row, 1968) 366, and *Theology of the New Testament*, II, tr. by Kendrick Grobel (New York: Scribner's 1955) 116–17 and C. K. Barrett, *Luke the Historian in Recent Study* (Philadelphia: Fortress, 1970) 9–15, 58–61, 63, 72. Bultmann and Barrett suggest that Luke is self-consciously a biographer-historian. Yet, as Barrett points out, Luke has carefully chosen to present only certain events and often his version of an event stands at odds with other well known sources. This difference in perspective may not point to an inferior Lucan source but to Luke's own understanding of the historical situation and to his concern for the needs of his congregation.
3 H. Conzelmann, *The Theology of St. Luke*, tr. by Geoffrey Buswell (New York: Harper and Row, 1960); H. Flender, *St Luke: Theologian of Redemptive History*, tr. by Reginald and Ilse Fuller (Philadelphia: Fortress, 1967); E. Haenchen, *The Acts of the Apostles*, tr. from 14th edition by Bernard Noble and Gerald Shinn, with the translation revised by R. McL. Wilson (Philadelphia: Westminster, 1971); J. C. O'Neill, *The Theology of Acts in Its Historical Setting* (London: SPCK, 1979); W. C. Robinson, Jr, *The Way of the Lord* (Basel: Universitätsverlag, 1960).
  As these authors point out, geography is also a constituent part of Luke's theology for he views history, apology and eschatology progressing along 'the Way of the Lord,' from Jerusalem the center of the religious world, the *urbs sancta*, to Rome the center of the political world, the *civitas aeterna*. Also

cf. H. Chadwick, 'The Circle and the Ellipse: Rival Concepts of Authority in the Early Church,' *Jerusalem and Rome* (Philadelphia: Fortress, 1966) 21–37.

4 F. C. Baur, 'Über Zweck und Veranlassung des Römerbriefs und die damit zusammenhängenden Verhältnisse der römischen Gemeinde,' *TZT* 1836, Heft 3, 100–14; 'Über den Ursprung des Episcopats,' *TZT* 1938, Heft 3, 142–3; *Paulus, der Apostel Jesu Christi*, I Teil (Leipzig: Fues, 1866) 7–18. On the relationship of Baur to Griesbach and Paulus, I am indebted to the excellent article by A. C. McGiffert, 'The Historical Criticism of Acts in Germany,' *The Beginnings of Christianity*, II, ed. by F. J. Foakes Jackson and K. Lake (London: Macmillan, 1922; hereafter designated *BC*) 363–95, a bibliographic treasury of nineteenth-century scholarship on the Lucan literature. Also cf. Haenchen, *Acts*, 15–49 and W. Gasque, 'The Historical Value of the Book of Acts,' *The Evangelical Quarterly* XLI (1969) 68–88.

5 K. Schrader, *Der Apostel Paulus*, Teil V (Leipzig: Christian Ernst Hollmann, 1836) 573–4.

6 M. Schneckenburger, *Über den Zweck der Apostelgeschichte* (Bern: Christian Fischer, 1841); cf. A. J. Mattill, 'The Purpose of Acts: Schneckenburger Reconsidered,' *Apostolic History and the Gospel*, ed. by W. Gasque and R. P. Martin (Grand Rapids, MI: Eerdmans, 1970) 108–22.

The corollary issue raised by the tendency critics questioned the historical accuracy of Acts. Baur felt that one was obligated to be skeptical about much of the history presented by the author of Acts because his primary purposes, conciliation and apology, would tend to distort people and events. Those who responded to Baur could be found on either side of his position. Schneckenburger, for example, was sure that Acts presented no serious deviation from historical fact while Schwegler (*Das Nachapostolische Zeitalter in den Hauptmomenten seiner Entwicklung*, II [Tübingen: Fues, 1846] 73–6, 106–18) was convinced that because Acts was so strongly apologetic, its value as history was nil.

7 E. Zeller, *The Contents and Origin of the Acts of the Apostles*, II, tr. by Joseph Dare (London: Williams and Norgate, 1875) 113–39.

8 Zeller, *Contents*, 161–5.

9 For example, B. Bauer, *Die Apostelgeschichte, eine Ausgleichung des Paulinismus und des Judenthums innerhalb der christlichen Kirche* (Berlin: G. Hempel, 1850).

10 Mattill, 'Purpose,' 113.

11 W. G. Kümmel, P. Feine and J. Behm, *Introduction to the New Testament*, tr. by A. J. Mattill (Nashville, TN: Abingdon, 1966) 144, my emphasis.

12 J. Weiss, *Über die Absicht und den literarischen Charakter der Apostel-Geschichte* (Marburg: Vandenhoeck and Ruprecht, 1897) 57.

13 *Ibid.*, 56–60.

14 Though Weiss' contribution to our understanding of Luke's purpose has been great, it should also be noted that some forty years earlier Zeller made almost the same statement about Luke's political apologetic: 'When it is added that in our book [Acts] account is taken precisely of those reproaches against Christianity which make it appear politically dangerous and contrary to law, the charge of introducing a prohibited cultus to the prejudice of the national religion, of revolutionary tendencies (the *Christiani hostes Caesarum*), there is every probability that the author, with his accumulation of stories of the rejection of these accusations by the pagan authorities, was endeavoring to refute the political suspicions against Christianity ...' (*Contents*, 163).

15 W. Ramsay, *St. Paul the Traveller and the Roman Citizen* (New York: Putnam, 1896) 308.
16 H. Sahlin, *Der Messias und das Gottesvolk* (ASNU 12; Uppsala: Almqvist and Wiksells, 1945) 35–6, 39–41.
17 For example see F. F. Bruce, *The Acts of the Apostles* (London: Tyndale, 1951) 30–1; G. B. Caird, *The Gospel of St. Luke* (Baltimore: Penguin, 1964) 14; F. C. Grant, *The Gospels: Their Origin and Growth* (New York: Harper, 1957) 119–29; A. Ehrhardt, *The Acts of the Apostles* (Manchester: Manchester University Press, 1969) Chs. 7 and 10; Foakes-Jackson and Lake, *BC* II, 177–87; and B. S. Easton, 'The Purpose of Acts,' *Early Christianity* (Greenwich, CT: Seabury, 1954).

One ought to note that other apologetic motifs have been seen imbedded in the Lucan literature. C. K. Barrett and C. Talbert have suggested that Luke attempted to rescue Paul from the gnostics (Barrett, *Luke the Historian*, 62–3 and Talbert, *Luke and the Gnostics* [Nashville: Abingdon, 1966] 14, 111–15).

J. C. O'Neill concludes that 'Luke–Acts was primarily an attempt to persuade educated Romans to become Christians; it was an 'apology' in outward form but, like all true apologies, it had the burning inner purpose of bringing men to faith. The use of the term 'apology' does not imply that Acts was chiefly designed to gain official recognition for Christianity' (*Theology of Acts*, 168). Luke was not on the defensive; rather, Luke's apology 'was to lead an educated reading public to embrace the Christian faith' (176). All other purposes are secondary to this including the demonstration that Christians are innocent of any revolutionary political tendencies.

Finally, A. Harnack, (*The Mission and Expansion of Christianity*, I, tr. by J. Moffatt [New York: G. P. Putnam, 1908] 259–60) and A. Plummer (*The Gospel According to St. Luke* [Edinburgh: T. & T. Clark, 1896] xxxvi) have suggested that Luke probably had no apologetic purpose at all. For further discussion see below, pp. 11ff.
18 H. J. Cadbury, *The Making of Luke–Acts* (London: SPCK, 1927; reprinted 1968; hereafter designated *MLA*) 302.
19 Cadbury, *MLA*, 303–4.
20 Cadbury, *MLA*, 308; Cadbury rightly and carefully qualifies his conjecture: 'Our knowledge of Roman law on these points and of Rome's treatment of the Christians in the first century is too uncertain for any assurance.'
21 Cadbury, *MLA*, 311.
22 *Ibid.*
23 Cadbury, *MLA*, 312–13.
24 Cadbury, *MLA*, 313.
25 *Ibid.*
26 *Ibid.*
27 Cadbury, *MLA*, 315. Vernon Robbins has recently revived this thesis. ('Prefaces in Greco-Roman Biography and Luke–Acts,' *SBL 1978 Seminar Papers*, II [Missoula, MT: Scholars Press, 1978] 193–207). He suggests that there is a linguistic parallel between the letters and speeches in the last half of Acts (15–28) and Luke's preparatory address to Theophilus. Robbins cites such words as δοκῶ (Acts 15:22, 25, 28; 25:27), γράφω (15:23; 18:28; 25:26 twice), πρᾶγμα (15:29; 25:11, 25), ἀκριβῶς (18:25, 26; 24:22), κατηχῶ (18:25; 21:21, 24), ἐπιγινώσκω (23:28; 24:8, 11; 25:10), ἀσφαλής (25:26), and κράτιστος (23:26; 24:3; 26:25).

Such a word distribution, however, proves little. Most of these words, and others from Luke's preface, occur elsewhere in the Third Gospel and in the first half of Acts; several words in the preface occur only there.

Robbins' conclusion that 'the preface introduces a relationship between Luke and Theophilus that parallels the relationship between Paul and Festus in Acts' (206) is hardly warranted either from what we know of Festus as Luke presents him, or from what we know of Theophilus, which is nothing (even Luke's use of κράτιστος proves nothing; cf. Cadbury, *MLA* 315). Robbins is among the latest to succumb to the traditional view that Luke writes a defense (though couched in 'didactic biography') of the church to a Roman official, identified as Theophilus.

28 H. J. Cadbury, 'The Purpose Expressed in Luke's Preface,' *Expositor* XXI, 126 (1921) 439. Also see Cadbury, 'Commentary on the Preface of Luke,' *BC*, II, App. C.

29 Cadbury, *MLA*, 12–17.

30 R. Bultmann, *Theology of the New Testament*, II, 116–17.

31 H. Conzelmann, *Die Mitte der Zeit* (Tübingen: Mohr, 1953; English translation, *The Theology of St Luke*). One should also remember that in 1920 H. J. Cadbury used the redaction critical method as a tool for understanding the Lucan literature; *The Style and Literary Method of Luke* (Cambridge, MA: Harvard University, 1920).

32 Conzelmann, *Luke*, 137.

33 Conzelmann, *Luke*, 148.

34 Conzelmann, *Luke*, 139.

35 Conzelmann, *Luke*, 140.

36 Conzelmann, *Luke*, 141.

37 Conzelmann, *Luke*, 142–4. Here Conzelmann parts company with Weiss. Much of Paul's defense centers on his attempt to differentiate two types of law, Roman and Jewish, and then to claim innocence with respect to both. Paul *must* make this clarification because 'the Jews deliberately present their accusations ambiguously' (143).

38 Ernst Haenchen, for example, comes to many of the same conclusions as Conzelmann. In the last quarter of Acts, Luke presents the Christian mission as politically benign; Rome, therefore, ought not be drawn into a Jewish sectarian conflict. Haenchen, however, revives Weiss' thesis that Luke wanted Christianity to be recognized as a *religio licita* (*Acts*, 630–1, 691–4; 'Judentum und Christentum in der Apostelgeschichte,' *ZNTW* LIV [1963] 186). J. Fitzmyer, in his recent commentary, offers this same view of Luke's apologetic perspective, in so far as there is one to be found in Luke–Acts. Luke has emphasized the historical relationship between Judaism and Christianity as a '*religio licita* ... to borrow a term from Tertullian'; *The Gospel According to Luke (I–IX)* (AB; Garden City, NY: Doubleday, 1981) 178–9, cf. 10.

Also see W. Marxsen, *Introduction to the New Testament*, tr. by G. Buswell (Philadelphia: Fortress, 1968) 159; H. Flender, *St. Luke*, 56–62; W. C. Robinson, Jr, *The Way of the Lord*, 81; W. Grundmann, *Das Evangelium nach Lukas* (THNT; Berlin: Evangelische Verlagsanstalt, 1971) 30–1; R. P. C. Hanson, *The Acts* (Oxford: Clarendon Press, 1967) 3–4.

39 H. Conzelmann, 'Luke's Place in the Development of Early Christianity,' *SLA*, 301.

40 Conzelmann, *Luke*, 137.
41 Conzelmann, *Luke*, 144. Cf. H. Conzelmann, *Die Apostelgeschichte* (HNT; Tübingen: Mohr, 1963) 10; also see Conzelmann's review of Haenchen in *TLZ* LXXXV (1960) 244–5.
42 Conzelmann, *Luke*, 142, my emphasis.
43 See below pp. 64–5. R. Karris, 'Missionary Communities: A New Paradigm for the Study of Luke–Acts,' *CBQ* XLI (1, 1979). Also see W. Radl, *Paulus und Jesus im lukanischen Doppelwerk* (Frankfort: H. Lang, 1975) 339–42; E. Ellis, *The Gospel of Luke* (rev. edition, London: Marshall, Morgan and Scott, 1974) 58–60; R. P. C. Hanson, *Acts*, 28–35.
44 Karris, 'Missionary Communities,' 86.
45 *Ibid.*
46 *Ibid.*, 87.
47 See below, Chapter 3.
48 J. M. Creed, *The Gospel According to St. Luke* (London: Macmillan, 1930) lxxii.
49 E. Franklin, *Christ the Lord*, 92–3.
50 *Ibid.*, 134–6. This assumes, of course, that Luke knew the outcome of Paul's trial. See below, pp. 18–21 and notes, on the date of composition for Luke's literature. Also see Hanson, *Acts*, 33.
51 Franklin, *Christ the Lord*, 137.
52 G. Schneider, 'Der Zweck des lukanischen Doppelwerks,' *BZ* XXI (1977) 60–61; W. Radl, *Paulus und Jesus*, 339–45.
53 R. Cassidy, *Jesus, Politics, and Society*, 129–30.
54 In Luke's schema Herod, the 'half-Jew,' stands half-way between imperial Rome and Palestinian Jewry. While he is not responsible for Jesus' death, he is responsible for Jesus' humiliation; see below, pp. 42–4.
55 Matt. 14:3–12; Mark 6:17–29; Jos. *Ant.* 18:116–19.
56 See below, pp. 36–7.
57 F. W. Danker is among the latest commentators struggling to harmonize such passages as Jesus' command to buy swords (22:36) with a political defense of Christianity aimed at a Roman official, Theophilus; *Jesus and the New Age* (St. Louis: Clayton Publishing House, 1972).

2. The politics of Luke: a reappraisal

1 Scholars continue to speculate about the identity of Theophilus. If he were a Roman magistrate, this would almost certainly indicate that Luke wrote a defense of the church. That Theophilus was a Roman, let alone a Roman magistrate, is not proven by Luke's language. One of the best treatments of Luke's preface was done by H. J. Cadbury, 'Commentary on the Preface of Luke,' *BC*, II, App. C; and 'The Purpose Expressed in Luke's Preface,' *Expositor* 8/XXI, 126 (1921) 439–40. Also see D. J. Sneen, 'An Exegesis of Luke 1:1–4 with Special Regard to Luke's Purpose as a Historian,' *Exp* LXXXIII (1971) 40–3.

E. Haenchen argues that the contents of Luke–Acts would make sense only to one familiar with the synagogue or church, which does not rule out someone well disposed to Christianity (*Acts*, 137, n. 4.). One should also note the considerable difficulty Haenchen has in identifying Luke's intended audience (compare *Acts*, 116 ['the Roman authorities'] and 'The Book of Acts as Source

Material for the History of Early Christianity,' *SLA*, 260 ['a more or less non-literary congregation']).

Schuyler Brown, on the other hand, is perhaps overly cautious in his assessment of the prologues ('The Role of the Prologues in Determining the Purpose of Luke–Acts,' *Perspectives on Luke–Acts*, ed. by C. Talbert [Danville, VA.: Association of Baptist Professors of Religion, 1978] hereafter designated *PLA*). Brown (following Talbert, *Luke and the Gnostics*, Ch. 7) lists five options for the purpose of Luke:

(1) The rehabilitation of Paul
(2) An apology directed to the Roman state
(3) The evangelization of the non-Christian world
(4) The solution of a theological problem
(5) A defense against heresy

I would add another which seems all too obvious: teaching within the church, the transmission of Christian tradition.

Each of these alternatives has recently been explored with varying degrees of plausibility. Brown, in fact, has shown that one could support any of these purposes by means of the prologues. An analysis of the prologues, therefore, is not sufficient for determining Luke's purpose.

2 G. H. P. Thompson, *The Gospel According to Luke* (Oxford: Oxford University Press, 1972) 11, and R. P. C. Hanson, *Acts*, 3–5, are recent typical examples.

3 There may have been other Zealots among the disciples; see O. Cullmann, *The State in the New Testament* (New York: Scribner's, 1956) 14–17 and M. Hengel, *Die Zeloten* (Leiden: Brill, 1961) 72–3.

4 Mark 3:17; also 5:41; 7:34; 15:22, 34.

5 S. G. F. Brandon, *The Fall of Jerusalem and the Christian Church* (London: SPCK, 1951) 207, 220; *The Trial of Jesus of Nazareth* (New York: Stein and Day, 1968) 78; *Jesus and the Zealots* (New York: Scribner's, 1967) 286–90.

6 F. J. Foakes Jackson and K. Lake, 'The Zealots,' *BC* I, App. A, 424–5.

7 Acts 21:20; 22:3.

8 Luke 6:15; Josephus, *JW* 2.651; 4.161; 7.268. One also wonders if Luke, in listing the apostles of the early church, might not have been influenced by similar lists of Jewish war heroes circulating at the time of his writing. Compare the order *'Simon*, the so-called *Zealot*, and *Judas* the son of James' (6:15; Acts 1:13) with the 'two Zealot brothers, *Simon* and *Judas*' which also closes the list of Josephus in *JW* 6.92 (cf. 6.148). There can be no doubt that Luke knew of a rebel movement in Palestine for in Acts 5:37 Luke accurately connects the revolt-provoking census of AD 6 with the rise of Judas the Galilean.

9 Acts 1:6–14.

10 There have been three interpretations usually given this difficult passage.
    (1) Literal: Jesus gave a command to take up arms against the oppressors (R. Eisler, *The Messiah Jesus and John the Baptist*, tr. by A. H. Krappe [New York: Dial Press, 1931] 368–70; Brandon, *Zealots*, 340–341; and Easton, *Luke*, 329).
    (2) Metaphorical: Jesus spoke metaphorically about the coming dangers for the church but the disciples reacted literally (J. M. Creed, *Gospel According to Luke*, 270; Conzelmann, *Luke*, 81–2, 233; Grundmann, *Das Evangelium*, 409; and I. H. Marshall, *The Gospel of Luke* [Exeter: Paternoster, 1978] 825).

(3) Restricted: though Jesus did issue the command, he intended the use of the arms to be far more restrained than the Zealots would have liked (Flender, *St. Luke*, 84 and Cullmann, *State*, 31).

Those who hold a literal interpretation of this passage, especially Eisler and Brandon, do not take sufficiently seriously the other side of Jesus' message of love even towards the enemy nor do they understand the apologetical intent of Luke's gospel. On the other hand, those who tend to spiritualize away the command, particularly Conzelmann, neglect the fact that the passage links the sword with the other concrete necessities of life (the bag, purse, and mantle) and they tend not to note the dangerous consequences which that command contained; Conzelmann never mentions that the command preludes the encounter in the garden.

11 That Luke included this command suggests an important piece of tradition which linked these words of Jesus with a scriptural pericope: 'And he was reckoned with transgressors' (Isa. 53:12). For the first-century Christian reader, this prophetic statement is fulfilled only a few lines later as Jesus is arrested by the chief priests and their soldiers on the Mount of Olives.

12 E. Franklin, *Christ the Lord*, 49–55; also see I. H. Marshall, *Luke: Historian and Theologian* (Grand Rapids: Zondervan, 1971) 162–7.

13 Also in Acts 17:7 Christians are accused of loyalty to 'another king, Jesus,' an accusation nowhere denied.

14 Compare Luke's non-eschatological presentation with Matt. 19:28.

15 Marshall suggests that while Jesus 'is the destined king during His earthly ministry,' it was the entry of Jesus into kingly power at his ascension that was significant for Luke (*Luke: Historian and Theologian*, 90).

16 A. Harnack, *The Acts of the Apostles*, tr. by J. R. Wilkinson (London: Williams and Norgate, 1909) 38–44. If this be the solution, then at most one can say that Luke has left a tantalizing, yet carefully ended legacy. The book of Acts hints at things to come for Paul and concludes with an appropriate sense of drama and literary polish. Luke chose well his time to die.

17 F. Pfister, 'Die zweimalige römische Gefangenschaft und die spanische Reise des Apostels Paulus und der Schluss der Apostelgeschichte,' *ZNTW* XIV (1913) 216–21. Perhaps death does not explain the ending. It may be that a later scribe excised the original ending of Acts which told of additional experiences of Peter that paralleled the *Acta Pauli*. According to Pfister (*op. cit.*), in order to render the apocryphal acts authoritative, the rival ending of the canonical Acts was removed. Against this theory, Cadbury notes that 'the last sentence of the book is too formal to have been left there merely as the result of mutilation, and too Lucan to be a subsequent redactor's patching. It has also been pointed out that as they stand, Luke and Acts are volumes of almost equal length, which suggests that the original author divided his material to fit a uniform and standard length of book roll, and planned them as they are' ('Roman Law and the Trial of Paul', *BC*, V, 337).

18 W. Ramsay, *St. Paul the Traveller and Roman Citizen*, 27–8, 309.

If Luke filled up a second volume, perhaps he planned or possibly wrote, a third, which would have resumed a narration of the acts of Peter and continued the story of both Peter and Paul, concluding with their martyrdoms. The use of πρῶτος ('first') instead of πρώτερος ('former') in Acts 1:1, cited as evidence that Luke intended a third book in the series (Ramsay, *St. Paul*, 27–8), makes the unwarranted assumption that he was strictly following the rules of classical grammar which would dictate the use of πρώτερος if only two volumes were projected, a former and a later (Haenchen, *Acts*, 137, n. 1.; K. Lake and H. J. Cadbury, *BC* IV, 349).

This theory has traditionally supposed that the third volume was (1) planned but not written, or (2) written but subsequently lost. An absent third volume does not help us resolve the questions we have raised about the political perspective implied by the ending of Acts.

A more potent suggestion about Luke's 'third volume' has recently been proposed in separate works by J. D. Quinn. ('The Last Volume of Luke: the Relation of Luke–Acts to the Pastoral Epistles,' *PLA*, 62–75, and S. G. Wilson (*Luke and the Pastoral Epistles* [London: SPCK, 1979]).

According to Quinn and Wilson, the Pastoral Epistles 'were the planned "third volume" of a trilogy' written shortly after (C. 90–95) the Acts of the Apostles. The epistles were composed not only to render additional information about the life of Paul, but to use the apostle's authority to counter the growing threat of gnosticism. Wilson, in particular, has provided us with a careful linguistic, political, ecclesiological, christological and theological comparison of Luke–Acts and the Pastorals. In many respects the two sets of works are very much alike, yet when we ask what this 'third volume' adds to our knowledge about the fate of Paul, one is compelled to conclude, not very much. The kind and quantity of information presented in this continuation of the life of Paul is as disappointing as the ending of Acts itself. The purpose of this 'third volume' cannot be a continued 'narrative of the things accomplished among us ... an orderly account' (Luke 1:1–2). Perhaps the Pastorals are, as Quinn maintains, an epistolary appendix for Luke–Acts, complementing and supplementing the narrative of Acts while rehabilitating the Pauline apostolate and teaching. While this proposal certainly supports my own contention that Theophilus was not a Roman magistrate passing judgment on the political point of view of the early church, neither does it offer much more than compounded speculation about why Luke *still* leaves Paul's fate to doubt.

The Pastoral Epistles only allow us to conjecture that Paul was released after his first Roman imprisonment (2 Tim. 4:16–17), that he resumed his missionary activity (Tit. 1:5; 3:12; cf. 1 Tim. 3:14), and that he was re-incarcerated to await martyrdom in depressing loneliness (2 Tim. 1:3–18; 2:9–10; 3:10–13; 4:6–22).

If the Pastoral Epistles are Luke's 'third volume,' then they support my thesis that Luke has presented a pro-Roman apologetic. Even in prison, Luke's 'Paul' can admonish his reader to offer 'supplications, prayers, intercessions, and thanksgivings ... for all men, for kings and all who are in high positions ...' (1 Tim. 2:1–2). He also charges Titus to remind his flock 'to be submissive to rulers and authorities' (Tit. 3:1–2).

It is interesting to note that a portion of Wilson's thesis rests on my own view of the political perspective of Luke–Acts: '... an interpretation that sees the primary audience as Christian readers makes far more sense of the rest of Luke–Acts. On this view the message would be that the Roman authorities are just and fair; they treat all citizens with impartiality and will not allow anyone to be arraigned on false charges. Christians have no need to fear civic authorities, and if they go on quietly with their business, Rome will leave them alone ...'

'Luke's motivation in taking up this stance was varied. One important factor
was the pragmatic observation that the Romans provided firm and orderly
government and thus encouraged a stable social and political environment in
which Christianity could expand. And, since on the whole the Romans were
fair in their treatment of the Church, confrontation with them would be both
useless and counter-productive' (*Luke and the Pastoral Epistles*, 39).

In all essentials, according to Wilson, Luke and the Pastor hold the same
attitude toward the state. This common political perspective need not, of course,
mean common authorship for Luke–Acts and the Pastorals. It could well be,
as I argue below, that Luke (and perhaps the author of the Pastorals) drew his
information about Paul's defense – and consequent political point of view –
from the apostle himself either by direct contact or by having access to his
Philippian correspondence (see pp. 51–2 and notes).

19   For a summary of the research see G. Ogg, *The Chronology of Paul* (London:
Epworth Press, 1968) 180–5. Also see O. Cullmann, *Peter: Disciple, Apostle,
Martyr*, tr. by F. Filson (rev. edition, Philadelphia: Westminster, 1962) 82–3,
93–110. A. Harnack, *The Date of the Acts and the Synoptic Gospels*, tr. by
J. R. Wilkinson (London: Williams and Norgate, 1911) 90–125; this was
Harnack's final statement about the ending of Acts. That Luke ceased to write
because he knew no more is a solution which usually intimates that Paul's case
had not yet been heard in Rome. Luke, therefore, must have written Acts (and
presumably the Third Gospel) at some time in the early sixties (though one
could also argue for a very late date; see below). J. A. T. Robinson has recently
re-opened the discussion about the date of Acts (*Redating the New Testament*
[Philadelphia: Westminster, 1976] 86–92; cf. B. Reicke, 'Synoptic Prophecies
on the Destruction of Jerusalem,' *Studies in the New Testament and Early
Christian Literature*, ed. by D. E. Aune [Leiden: Brill, 1972] 121–34; for a
convenient listing of evidence that supports an early date of composition see
F. F. Bruce, *Acts*, 11–13; E. J. Goodspeed presents the arguments for a later
dating of Luke–Acts in *Introduction to the New Testament* [Chicago:
University of Chicago, 1937] 191–7).

To Robinson's argument I would only add that if Paul was in Rome under
house arrest from 60–2, there is every likelihood that he would have been
treated well. Luke's optimism about Roman justice accurately reflects this
period of history. Nero's early reign was seen as one of enlightenment; he was
hailed as the 'new Augustus,' promising *clementia* even to those among the
lower social classes who had been previously judged as enemies of the state.
Paul's appeal to Caesar was not ill-placed (cf. Seneca, *Clem.* 1.2; Tacitus, *Ann.*
13.11, 26, 43; 14.45; Suetonius, *Nero* 10.2).

One could also conclude that Luke's ignorance about Paul's fate does not
require the supposition that Luke wrote in the early sixties. To say that Luke
stopped his narrative because he knew nothing further about Paul's life would
not lead me to conclude that Luke wrote before the conclusion of Paul's trial,
but long after. Assuming this option to be correct, if Luke was aware that Paul
lived in Rome for at least 'two whole years' why did he say nothing about the
progress of events *during* that time? Had his sources been so exhausted that he
was unable to reconstruct the story? Such a theory is neither supported by
Luke's customary use of vintage source material, nor very convincing in the
face of alternative explanations.

Perhaps it is the case that Luke, writing in the eighties or nineties, simply had no further reliable information about Paul. The apostle has disappeared into the mists of the Spanish moors. This suggestion proves to be less startling when we compare Luke's ending with Clement's mention of Paul (1 Clem. 5).

Clement of Rome implies that Paul was released from house arrest, and then carried his mission to the western limits of the empire. His report of Paul's fate is, like Luke's, vague: 'when he reached the limits of the West he gave his testimony before the rulers (μαρτυρήσας ἐπὶ τῶν ἡγουμένων) and thus passed from the world (οὕτως ἀπηλλάγη τοῦ κόσμου) and was taken up (ἀνελήμφθη) into the Holy Place ...' (1 Clem. 5.7; R. M. Grant and H. H. Graham suggest that for Clement 'the limits of the West' mean Cadiz and the Pillars of Hercules, *The Apostolic Fathers*, II [New York: Nelson, 1965] 26). Such mythical language does not increase confidence in the historicity of Clement's report. Also, one must ask why Clement, writing from the imperial capital, did not write a more detailed report of Paul's martyrdom (if indeed he was martyred in Rome)? Perhaps Clement, like Luke, simply knew no more about Paul. Cadbury points to parallel ambiguous endings of Philostratus' life of Apollonius and the author of Second Maccabees: *MLA*, 322. And yet, we are left with the nagging suspicion that Luke did know more about Paul than he reported. As I have already mentioned, Luke hints at Paul's martyrdom. Furthermore, it seems reasonable to assume that Luke would have known from information received from the Pauline churches, or through information maintained in the church at Rome, the result of Paul's trial.

20 Cf. Hanson, *Acts*, 34; Cadbury, *MLA*, 321-4; and F. Filson, 'The Journey Motif in Luke–Acts,' in *Apostolic History and the Gospel*, 75-7.

21 Cited in F. C. Cook, 'The Acts of the Apostles,' *The Bible Commentary* (New York: Scribner's, 1895) 534.

22 K. Lake, 'What was the End of St. Paul's Trial?' quoted in *BC* V, 326-32, cf. 331.

Early in this century K. Lake, W. M. Ramsay, and H. J. Cadbury proposed that Luke's mention of 'two years' (Acts 28:30) indicates that the case never came to trial; the statutory period of eighteen months had elapsed before Paul's accusers pursued the case in Rome (Ramsay, 'The Imprisonment and Supposed Trial of St. Paul in Rome,' *Expositor* 8/V [1913] 264-84; Cadbury, 'Roman Law and the Trial of Paul,' *BC*, V, 297ff.). T. Mommsen, however, had earlier recognized that the imperial edict on which Ramsay and Cadbury based their judgment belonged to the third century. The 'appeal' to which it refers is the *appellatio* against a sentence already passed, and not the first-century procedure of *provocatio* which prevented the court from completing a case in the face of an appeal (Mommsen, *Römisches Strafrecht* [Leipzig: Duncker und Humbolt, 1899] 469, n.1, 472, n.5, 473, n.1; Cadbury reproduces the document in 'Roman Law', 333-4; also see the important collection of essays by A. H. M. Jones, *Studies in Roman Government and Law* [New York: Praeger, 1960] especially 'Imperial and Senatorial Jurisdiction in the Early Principate,' 69-98, and 'I Appeal unto Caesar,' 53-65). A. H. M. Jones has concluded that from the date of the enactment (during the principate of Augustus) of the *lex Iulia de vi publica*, a magistrate invested with *imperium* or *potestas* was forbidden to scourge, chain, torture or execute a Roman citizen anywhere in the empire, or to sentence him if he appealed to Rome, or to prevent him from taking his case to Rome, except for cases which involved the breach of statute laws [*ordo*], which Paul's case [*extra ordinem*] did not; cf. A. N. Sherwin-White, *Roman Society and Roman Law in the New Testament* (Oxford: Oxford University Press, 1963) 63–70, 112–16; Haenchen, *Acts*, 724–6, n.3; P. Garnsey, 'The *Lex Iulia* and Appeal under the Empire,' *JRS* LVIII (1966) 182–7.

23 C. S. C. Williams, *The Acts of the Apostles* (HNTC; New York: Harper, 1957) 19.

24 P. Winter, *On the Trial of Jesus* (Berlin: De Gruyter, 1961) 86–7.

25 G. Miles and G. Trompf, 'Luke and Antiphon: The Theology of Acts 27–28 in the Light of Pagan Beliefs about Divine Retribution, Pollution, and Shipwreck,' *HTR* LXIX (1967) 265.

26 It is doubtful that Luke would have considered Paul's martyrdom any more of a defeat than the death of Jesus or Stephen; cf. R. J. Knowling, 'The Acts of the Apostles,' *The Expositor's Greek Testament*, II, ed. by W. R. Nicoll (New York: Dodd, Mead, & Co., 1900) 553.

27 Hanson, *Acts*, 33.

28 O. Cullmann, *Peter*, 102; also see C. K. Barrett, 'Pauline Controversies in the Post-Pauline Period,' *NTS* XX (1973–4) 234; and A. J. Mattill, 'The Purpose of Acts,' in *Apostolic History and The Gospel*, 121–2.

29 1 Clem. 4 (note Clement's OT examples); Phil. 1:15–17.

30 2 Cor. 11:26; cf. 12:19.

31 S. Wilson, *Luke and the Pastoral Epistles*, 113; cf. 2 Tim. 4:9–10, 16.

32 Williams, *The Acts of the Apostles*, 241; Haenchen, *Acts*, 614; cf. Lake and Cadbury, *BC* IV, 274.

33 Luke's note that the disaffected Jews were from Asia corresponds with the locus of trouble mentioned by Paul (1 Cor. 15:32; 16:8–9; 2 Cor. 1:8–10; cf. especially C. K. Barrett, *The Second Epistle to the Corinthians* [HNTC; New York: Harper, 1973] 63–5 and P. E. Hughes, *Paul's Second Epistle to the Corinthians* [Grand Rapids, MI: Eerdmans, 1962] 16–21. In 2 Cor. 1:8–10 we are reminded of the narrative of Acts 20 by such terms as $\theta\lambda\hat{\iota}\psi\iota\varsigma$, $\dot{\alpha}\pi\acute{o}\kappa\rho\iota\mu\alpha$, and the perfect tense verb $\dot{\epsilon}\sigma\chi\acute{\eta}\kappa\alpha\mu\epsilon\nu$; the decision against Paul remained in effect even after he left Asia (cf. Acts 20:22–3).

34 Cullmann contends that Jewish-Christians in Rome, during the Neronian persecution, pointed out Paul, along with other Christian leaders, to the magistrates; *Peter*, 106–7.

35 Acts 5:36–7. Dibelius contests the notion that Luke has inaccurately recollected Josephus (*BC* II, 356). The anachronism, along with the whole speech, is a product of Luke himself (*Studies*, 186–7).

36 Franklin, *Christ the Lord*, 137; also see D. Juel, *An Introduction to New Testament Literature* (Nashville: Abingdon, 1978) 221. Juel concludes that there is apologetic material in Acts which defends Paul's 'fidelity to Jewish tradition.' That the 'narrator seems little interested in the confrontation between Paul and the Roman authorities' (232) is contradicted by the space allocated the trial scenes as well as the technical details of imperial government so liberally scattered throughout Luke–Acts.

37 Franklin, *Christ the Lord*, 138.

38 Josephus, *Ant*. 18.85–7. Luke's picture of Pilate is far less acrimonious than the one Josephus paints: *Ant*. 18.55–62; *JW* 2.169–76.

39 Eisler, *The Messiah*, 500–10; Brandon, *Fall*, 106–107.
40 I shall return to this in Chapter 3, E.
41 C. Talbert, *Literary Patterns, Theological Themes and the Genre of Luke–Acts* (SBLMS 20; Missoula, MT: Scholars Press, 1974) 44–5; R. Brown, *The Birth of the Messiah* (Garden City, NY: Doubleday, 1977) 241–3, 408–12.
42 Among those who see a single source behind Luke 1–2 are W. L. Knox, *The Sources of the Synoptic Gospels*, ed. by H. Chadwick (Cambridge: Cambridge University Press, 1953) II, 40–3, and F. W. Goodman, 'Sources of the First Two Chapters in Matthew and Luke,' *CQR* CLXII (1961) 136–43. K. L. Schmidt, *Der Rahmen der Geschichte Jesu* (Berlin: Trowitzsch and Sohn, 1919) 309–14, suggested as many as seven sources in Luke 1–2. For an excellent recent review of source study see I. H. Marshall, *The Gospel of Luke*, 47–9; also see H. H. Oliver, 'The Lukan Birth Stories and the Purpose of Luke–Acts,' *NTS* X (1964) 205–15.
Raymond Brown concludes that one need not see Luke dependent on sources for the birth narrative. Rather, Luke has taken some items that came to him from tradition (the names of John the Baptist's parents, annunciation patterns from the Old Testament, the two canticles) and, using information about Jesus, Mary, and John the Baptist that occurs later in the Gospel, fashioned his own narrative (*The Birth of the Messiah*, 241–50; 'Luke's Method in the Annunciation Narrative of Chapter One,' *PLA*, 126–38). Brown's approach is most convincing with respect to the Lucan method. I think Brown is also correct in viewing Luke 1–2 as a Lucan bridge from the Old Testament to the life of Jesus, and Acts 1–2 as a parallel bridge between the life of Jesus and the history of the early church: *Birth*, 242.
43 W. L. Knox, *Some Hellenistic Elements in Primitive Christianity* (London: H. Milford, 1944) 9–10. Also Bultmann, *History*, 297 who otherwise thinks that Luke relied on source material, sees here the hand of Luke. On the other hand Dibelius (*Botschaft und Geschichte* [Tübingen: Mohr, 1953] I, 65) and Sahlin (*Der Messias*, 195) conclude that even in these verses Luke is dependent on a source.
44 It would be unwieldy to go through the detailed discussion of this very complex problem. I shall only refer the reader to some of the more important works beginning with E. Schürer's classical treatment, 'The Valuation Census of Quirinius,' *A History of the Jewish People in the Age of Jesus Christ* (Edinburgh: T. & T. Clark, rev. edition, 1973) I, 399–427. Updated reviews of the problem may be found in G. Ogg, 'The Quirinius Question Today,' *ExpT* LXXIX (1968) 231–6 and R. Brown, *Birth*, 547–55. Also, P. W. Barnett, '*Apographe* and *apographesthai* in Luke 2:1–5,' *ExpT* LXXXV (1973–4) 377–80; W. M. Ramsay, 'Luke's Narrative of the Birth of Jesus,' *Expositor* 8/IV (1912) 385–407, 481–507 and *Was Christ Born at Bethlehem?* (New York: Putnam, 1898) 95–248; A. N. Sherwin-White, *Roman Society*, 162–71; and I. H. Marshall, *The Gospel of Luke*, 99–104.
45 Luke 1:3, 5; 3:1–2; Acts 11:28; 12:1–3, 18–23; 18:12–17; 24:27–25:1.
46 This was Schürer's conclusion (*History of the Jewish People*, I, 426–7) more recently echoed by Creed, *Luke*, 28–30 and Cadbury, *MLA*, 327.
47 H. Braunert, 'Der römische Provinzialzensus und der Schätzungsbericht des Lukas-Evangeliums,' *Historia* VI (1957) 213–14. Also see W. L. Knox, *Some Hellenistic Elements*, 9–10.

48 W. Grundmann, *Das Evangelium nach Lukas*, 80.
49 H. Moehring, 'The Census in Luke as an Apologetic Device,' in *Studies in the New Testament and Early Christian Literature*, ed. by D. E. Aune (Brill: Leiden, 1972), 144–60.
50 Brown, *Birth*, 413.
51 *Res Gestae Divi Augusti* 12, 34.
52 Virgil, *Eclogues* 4.15–17.
53 The inscription at Halicarnassus cited in R. Brown, *Birth*, 415.
54 Brown, *Birth*, 415; a similar conclusion is reached by Danker, *Jesus*, 24.
55 I. H. Marshall, *The Gospel of Luke*, 109.
56 One might recall that when Luke is writing, the Augustan ideals, while they had been challenged by Caligula, had not faded from view. Even in the early years of Nero's reign, the infamous emperor was hailed as the new Augustus who would restore the blessings of that former golden age.
57 Josephus, *Ant.* 18.1–4, 9.
58 Marshall recounts four other commonly posed solutions to the problematic πρώτη: *The Gospel of Luke*, 98–9.
59 Luke considered the soldiers of Palestine (Judea) to be 'Romans' – not necessarily Roman citizens, but direct agents of the *imperium*. The next section (Jesus and the centurion) explores Luke's understanding of the Roman army in Palestine.
60 Grundmann (*Das Evangelium*, 103) suggests that Luke used his special source, Sahlin (*Der Messias*, 37) considers this to be from Q, and Bultmann (*History*, 145) thinks this to be a Lucan addition.
61 Luke 3:15; 4:42; 8:40.
62 Luke 5:3, 13; 6:19; 9:11, 16; 11:52; 19:48; 20:1.
63 Luke 13:17; 20:19, 26; 22:2.
64 Luke 23:13–18; cf. Luke 24:19–20, the people recognized Jesus to be a mighty prophet while their 'chief priests and rulers delivered him up to be condemned to death, and crucified him.'
65 Luke 23:48.
66 Luke 5:1–11, 27–8, 30, 33; 6:2; 19:39. J. B. Tyson has pointed out that Luke distinguishes between the Pharisaic challenge concerning the Torah and the chief priests' total opposition to Jesus. In Acts the Pharisees are presented in a favorable light; 'The Opposition to Jesus in the Gospel of Luke,' *Pers Rel Stud* V (1978) 144–50. Also see J. A. Ziesler, 'Luke and the Pharisees,' *NTS* XXV (1979) 146–57.
67 Acts 4:13.
68 Cf. Matt. 3:7. It is impossible to tell which text represents the Q source. Whether or not Luke found 'multitude' in his source, the word certainly served his purposes better than 'Pharisees and Sadducees.' The multitudes, not their leaders, hear the gospel and are baptized – a theme which recurs throughout the Third Gospel and Acts.
69 Luke 3:21; 7:29–33.
70 Ezek. 18:5–9, 14–16; Isa. 58:6–7; Job 31:16–22.
71 See the long list of citations from Cicero, Philo, Dio Cassius and Josephus in F. M. Heichelheim, 'Roman Syria,' *An Economic Survey of Ancient Rome*, IV, ed. Tenney Frank (Baltimore: Johns Hopkins University, 1938) 244, n.8.; 245, n.82.

72 Heichelheim, 'Roman Syria,' 245.
73 Cf. G. H. Stevenson, 'The Provinces and Their Government,' *Cambridge Ancient History* (Cambridge: University Press, 1932; hereafter *CAH*) IX, 469–71. Stevenson suggests that there was yet another way for the Syrian publicani to increase their profits; they would loan the company's capital to local magistrates, 'often at extortionate rates of interest, the sums which provincial communities owed to the government' (471).
74 G. H. Stevenson, 'The Imperial Administration,' *CAH*, X, 191. It should also be noted that the great tax-gathering companies of the Republic were nearly ruined as Pompey demanded most of their resources during the civil war. Furthermore, by denying them new territories, Augustus hindered them from recovering their losses.
75 Josephus, *Ant.* 14:190–206; cf. Schürer, *History of the Jewish People*, I, 372–6; Heichelheim, 'Roman Syria,' 233.
76 A. H. M. Jones, *A History of Rome Through the Fifth Century*, II. (New York: Walker, 1970) 256–62; H. Stuart Jones, 'Administration,' *The Legacy of Rome*, ed. by C. Bailey (Oxford: Clarendon Press, 1923) 117–18; N. Lewis and M. Reinhold, *Roman Civilization*, II (New York: Columbia University, 1955) 399–402.
77 Plummer, *Gospel According to Luke*, 92, indicates that the text [3:14] links the two groups together with καὶ ἡμεῖς. Lewis and Reinhold note that 'tax collectors were frequently accompanied on their rounds by armed guards or soldiers, whom they needed for protection but whom they often used to intimidate and maltreat the taxpayers' (*Roman Civilization*, 400, n. 205).
78 Matt. 9:10–11; 18:17; 21:31; Mark 2:15; Luke 5:30; 7:34; 15:1; 18:11; 19:9. Note how Luke (5:29), unlike Matt. (9:10), has modified his source to read 'tax-collectors and others.' The observation that Jesus eats with 'tax-collectors and sinners' is made by the Pharisees, not the Evangelist (5:30). Likewise, Luke amends his Q source so that the Matthean 'tax-collectors and Gentiles' are reduced to the ambiguity of 'sinners' (Matt. 5:46–7/Luke 6:32–3). Only at Luke 15:1 does the Evangelist himself group together tax-collectors and sinners, but the repeated article indicates that Luke considered them to be by no means identical; cf. Plummer, *Gospel According to Luke*, 368. Note also Luke's inclusion of the parable of the Pharisee and the publican at prayer (18: 9–14).
79 Josephus, *JW* 3.54–5; Pliny, *Nat. Hist.* 5.14.70 (a slightly different list which nevertheless retains Jericho as a toparchy). Cf. Schürer, *History of the Jewish People*, I, 372–6.
80 Luke 19:7.
81 Luke 3:8, cf. 19:40; 1 Pet. 2:4–5; Herm. Vis. 3.2.4ff.; 3.5.1ff; Sim. 9.3–13.
82 I. H. Marshall has suggested that these soldiers were 'not Roman, but the forces of Herod Antipas stationed in Peraea (possibly including non–Jews, like his father's army, Josephus, *Ant.* 17. 198–9), or perhaps Jewish auxiliaries used in Judea for police duties ...,' (*The Gospel of Luke*, 143). While foot-soldiers were provincials, the leadership of Herod's and Pilate's forces would have been composed of Romans.
83 Comp. John 19:2, 23–4, 32–4; Rev. 6:15; 19:18.
84 Luke 7:2; 23:47; Acts 10:1ff.; 22:25–6; 23:17, 23; 27:1ff.; 28:16. Haenchen notes that Luke makes it appear that Paul is the first to bring the

gospel to Rome, while in truth it had preceded him there "The Book of Acts as Source Material for the History of Early Christianity,' *SLA*, 278).

85 Acts 13:4–12; 16:35–40; 18:12–17; 19:30–1; 23:16–30. See W. H. C. Frend, *Martyrdom and Persecution in the Early Church* (Oxford: Blackwell, 1965) 159.

86 Luke 23:4, 14, 22; Acts 26:31. It was Paul's appeal to his citizenship and to the emperor that saved him from sharing his master's fate.

87 The British Museum papyrus number 1, 171 (AD 42) provides an interesting parallel:

> Lucius Aemilius Rectus [prefect of Egypt] declares:
> No one shall be permitted to requisition transportation facilities from the people in the country districts nor demand viatica or anything else gratis without a permit from me. ... But if any of the soldiers or police or anyone at all among the aides in the public services is reported to have acted in violation of my edict or to have used force against anyone of the country people or to have exacted money, I shall visit the utmost penalty upon him. Year 2 of the Emperor Tiberius Claudius Caesar Augustus, Germaniceus the 4th. (Cited in Lewis and Reinhold, *Roman Civilization*, II, 400–1.)

88 Heidland, *TDNT*, V, 591–2 notes that ὀψώνιον is the military technical term for a legally fixed rate of pay to be allotted in periodic (monthly) payments. This basic rate was accompanied by allowances in cash and kind; John the Baptist's message is against seizing by force these 'allowances.'

89 See my comments on the Lucan birth narrative, pp. 25–8. The virtues of the Augustan age, recorded in political (Plutarch, Dio Chrysostom) and poetical (Horace, Virgil) writings, propagated in intellectual circles, would not have been lost on an author such as Luke. Cf. S. Benko and J. O'Rourke, *The Catacombs and the Colosseum* (Valley Forge, PA: Judson Press, 1971); C. N. Cochrane, *Christianity and Classical Culture* (New York: Galaxy, 1957) 1–113; A. Grenier, *The Roman Spirit in Religion, Thought, and Art* (New York: Cooper Square Publishers, 1970 [1926]) 291–315; C. D. Morrison, *The Powers That Be* (Naperville, IL: Allenson, 1960); M. P. Nilsson, *Imperial Rome* (New York: Schocken, 1962) 3–64; E. Stauffer, *Christ and the Caesars*, tr. by K. and R. G. Smith (Philadelphia: Westminster, 1952).

90 According to Luke, the leaders of the Jews also have authority, the 'authority of darkness' (Luke 22:53).

91 Marshall, *The Gospel of Luke*, 277–8, summarizes the arguments about Luke's relationship to Q; also see Bultmann, *History*, 68.

92 Easton, *Luke*, 95; W. F. Burnside, *The Gospel According to St. Luke* (Cambridge: Cambridge University Press, 1913) 135; F. Godet, *Commentary on the Gospel of St Luke*, tr. by E. W. Shalders and M. D. Cusin (Edinburgh: T. & T. Clark, 1870) 337; H. K. Luce, *The Gospel According to St. Luke* (Cambridge: Cambridge University Press, 1936) 152; W. Manson, *The Gospel of Luke* (MNTC; New York: R. R. Smith, 1930) 75; Plummer, *Gospel According to Luke*, 194; and Caird, *Gospel of Luke*, 108.

93 Tiberias would have been a more likely place of residence for an army officer. Luke is sufficiently vague (compare Luke 7:1–2 with Matthew 8:5) to leave this possibility open.

94 φοβούμενοι τὸν θεόν: Acts 10:2, 22; 13:16; σεβόμενοι τὸν θεόν: Acts 13:43;
16:14; 18:7; cf. Josephus, *Ant.* 14.110; προσήλυτος: Acts 2:11; 6:5; 13:43.
Also see K. Lake, 'Proselytes and God-fearers,' *BC*, V, 74–96.

95 A. D. Nock, 'The Augustan Restoration,' *Essays on Religion in The Ancient
World*, I, ed. by Z. Stewart (Oxford: Clarendon Press, 1972) 16–25. Also see
A. D. Nock, 'Religious Developments from the Close of the Republic to the
Death of Nero,' *CAH*, X, 475–80; A. Grenier, *The Roman Spirit*, 365–85;
Lewis and Reinhold, *Roman Civilization*, II, 55–65, 78–9; J. Ferguson, *The
Religions of the Roman Empire* (Ithaca, NY: Cornell University, 1970) 72–6.

96 Sherwin-White, *Roman Society*, 124; other recent commentators rely on
Sherwin-White at this point, e.g. Marshall, *The Gospel of Luke*, 143, 279.

97 Cf. Josephus, *JW* 2.51–65.

98 F. Blass and A. DeBrunner, *A Greek Grammar of the New Testament and
Other Early Christian Literature*, tr. by R. Funk (Chicago: University of
Chicago, 1961; hereafter *BD*) 5.3b.

99 Cf. Luce, *Gospel According to Luke*, 153; Caird, *Gospel of Luke*, 108, claims
that the centurion was commissioned by Antipas.

100 J. Jeremias, *Jerusalem in the Time of Jesus*, tr. by F. H. and C. H. Cave (Philadelphia: Fortress, 1969) 299; Josephus, *JW* 3.70.

101 There were four categories of military officers: legate, prefect, tribune, and
centurion. For a full discussion of the military system, how appointments
were made, and the life of Roman soldiery see H. M. D. Parker, *The Roman
Legions* (Oxford: Clarendon Press, 1928) 185–211 and M. P. Nilsson, *Imperial
Rome*, 281–316. Also see Polybius' description of the republican army (A. H.
M. Jones, *The Later Roman Empire*, I [Oxford: Blackwell, 1964] 197–202),
the articles on the imperial army in Jones, *The Later Roman Empire*, II, 148–
77, G. Webster, *The Roman Imperial Army of the First and Second Centuries
AD* (New York: Funk & Wagnalls, 1969), and Josephus' excellent description
in *JW* 3.70–109.

102 Parker, *The Roman Legions*, 189.

103 Nilsson, *Imperial Rome*, 304; Parker, *The Roman Legions*, 224; cf. Jones,
The Later Roman Empire, II, 152.

104 Luke is fond of the terms φιλία, ἄξιος, ἐξουσία, σέβομαι, εὐσεβής. In this Q
story he has added the notion of friendship (cf. Luke 14:10; 16:9; 23:12;
Acts 10:24; 19:31), and expanded on the themes of worthiness and authority
(cf. Luke 5:24; 15:19, 21; Acts 1:7; 9:14; 26:10). On φιλία as a virtue for those
in authority, see Plutarch, *Praec. ger. reip.* 18 and Dio Chrysostom, *Or.* 1.21–22.
Even though Luke carefully reports the words of his source about the faith
(πίστις) of the centurion, the passage in Acts 18:7–8 makes it apparent that he
considers 'having faith' (ἐπίστευσεν τῷ κυρίῳ) and 'being pious' (σεβομένου
τὸν θεόν) to be synonomous (compare Luke 7:4–5, 9 with Acts 10:1–2, 22;
cf. Epict. 3.7.26; Philo, *Virt.* 34, 216; *Leg. All.* 3.209, 229; *Spec.* 4.187–8).
A. D. Nock and others point to Virgil's *Aeneid* as the apotheosis of Roman
religious expression, the heart of which was *pietas*, the sense of duty to family,
state, and the protective deities. Personal inclinations were best sacrificed on
the altar of duty to the larger order which finds its embodiment in the person
of the emperor. While the emperor ruled the realm by his *auctoritas*, *pietas*
was the religious expression of respect for the binding power of the emperor's
authority. See A. D. Nock, 'Religious Developments from the Close of the

Republic to the Death of Nero,' *CAH*, X, 465–511; W. W. Fowler, 'Religious
Feeling in the Poems of Virgil,' Lecture XVIII, *The Religious Experience of the
Roman People* (London: Macmillan, 1911) 403–27; C. N. Cochrane, *Christianity
and the Classical Culture*, 19–26, 61–73. Also, M. P. Charlesworth, 'Some
Observations on the Ruler-Cult, Especially in Rome,' *HTR* XXVIII (1935);
A. D. Nock, 'The Emperor's Divine *Comes*,' *Essays in Religion in the Ancient
World*, II, 653ff.

105 This *Today's English Version* translation has captured the mood of the discussion
between Jesus and the centurion.

106 See Fitzmyer, *Luke*, 652.

107 Acts 10. Perhaps Conzelmann is correct that the 'time of the church' must come
after Jesus has completed his earthly mission (*Luke*, 14–17, 209–13); therefore,
the miracle which Jesus performs for the 'centurion' (a paradigm of an interested
Roman authority) prepares him for conversion by the apostles. In the Third
Gospel the centurion is a pagan Roman who 'loves the nation'; in Acts 10:2,
22, the centurion has become religious, righteous, a God-fearer (εὐσεβής,
δίκαιος, φοβούμενος τὸν θεόν), and eventually a Christian. See also W. Schmithals,
Das Evangelium nach Lukas (Zürich: Theologischer Verlag, 1980) 91–2.

108 Acts 10:28.

109 Acts 10:2, 22. Cornelius was also a centurion of the auxiliary troops, the
'Italian cohort,' σπείρης 'Ιταλικῆς, there being no legionary forces in Judea at
the time. The auxiliaries were known by their *natio* while the legionnaires
were designated by their native town. Sherwin-White, *Roman Society*, 160;
Parker, *The Roman Legions*, 185.

110 Acts 10:25. Luke's language in this vignette is powerful. Προσκύνησις was an
act of obeisance reserved for divine beings and human authorities of the highest
order. A Roman centurion of the Italian cohort lying prone before a Galilean
peasant would certainly make exciting reading for the Christian community.
One might ask, however, what a Roman magistrate might have thought of such
a scene. See H. Greeven, '*proskyneo, proskynetes*', *TDNT*, VI, 758–66; L. R.
Taylor, *The Divinity of the Roman Emperor* (Middletown, CT: American
Philological Association, 1931, reprinted 1975) esp. 247–66.

111 Also see Cassidy, *Jesus, Politics, and Society*, 55–61, for a most confusing
exegesis that vacillates between speculation about what Jesus meant by his
response and how Luke interpreted this response. J. S. Kennard, in an older
study, wisely distinguishes Jesus' response (anti-Roman, according to Kennard)
from Luke's more conciliatory stance; *Render to God: A Study of the Tribute
Passage* (New York: Oxford University Press, 1950) 129–39.

112 Rom. 13:1–7; 1 Pet. 2:13–17; Seneca, *Clem.* 1.5.6–7; Plutarch, *Max. cum
princ. phil. esse diss.* 1; *Ad princ. ineru.* 3; Dio Chr., *Or.* 1.15, 42–6; 2.75;
Josephus, *JW* 3.353–4; 5.366–8, 376–8; Philo, see the fragment quoted by
E. R. Goodenough, *The Politics of Philo Judaeus* (New Haven, CT: Yale
University, 1938) 99; and 1 Clem. 60.4–61.2.

113 Philo suggested that even tyrants rule by the providence of God. Their function
was to chastise and to purge the human race when wickedness grows so great
that God must intervene through human channels. Just as the state must maintain executioners to deal with murderers, so must God from time to time allow
tyrants to have dominion over nations; *Prov.* 11.37–41; cf. Rom. 13:3–5;
Seneca, *Clem.* 1.11–24; also see C. K. Barrett, 'The New Testament Doctrine
of Church and State,' *New Testament Essays* (London: SPCK, 1972) 12–15.

114 Ellis, *The Gospel of Luke*, 234.
115 Danker, *Jesus*, 203.
116 For example see C. J. Cadoux, *The Early Church and the World* (Edinburgh: Clark, 1925) 168; A. D. Nock, 'Soter and Euergetes,' *The Joy of Study*, ed. by Sherman E. Johnson (New York: Macmillan, 1951) 136; and Sherwin-White, *Roman Society*, 137.
117 Cullmann, *State*, 19.
118 W. Manson, *Luke*, 244; Creed, *Gospel According to Luke*, 267; Plummer, *Gospel According to Luke*, 501.
119 A philosophy echoed by Plutarch, *Ad princ. ineru.* 3 and Dio Chr., *Or* 1.21.
120 Easton, *Luke*, 324; also see Marshall, *The Gospel of Luke*, 812.
121 W. Bauer, *A Greek–English Lexicon of the New Testament and Other Early Christian Literature*, tr. and adapted by W. Arndt and F. W. Gingrich (Chicago: University of Chicago, 1957) 422, suggests that κατεξουσιάζω may mean 'tyrannize.' Though the word is unattested in the LXX, Josephus, or Philo, we can conclude with Foerster (*TDNT*, II, 575) that 'the word implies the tendency towards compulsion or oppression which is immanent in all earthly power.' Also see K. W. Clark, 'The Meaning of [Kata] kyrieuein,' in *Studies in New Testament Language and Text*, ed. by J. K. Elliott (Leiden: Brill, 1976) 100–5. Clark argues that both κυριεύειν and κατακυριεύειν should be translated 'to rule over, to exercise lordship over, to be lord of, to master, to have dominion over' rather than 'to lord it over.' His argument, however, relates to modern translations of the term rather than the nuance Luke may have intended.
122 Vincent Taylor suggested that Luke did not use Mark as a source. According to Taylor, of the 67 words in Luke 22:24–7, only 21 are in common with Mark. Even though Taylor notes that in Luke 22:25–6a fifteen of twenty words are shared, it is 'not very probable that Luke is borrowing from Mark' (*Behind the Third Gospel: a Study of the Proto-Luke Hypothesis* [Oxford: Clarendon Press, 1926] 41–2). In his last book Taylor held essentially the same position; *The Passion Narrative of St. Luke*, ed. by O. E. Evans (SNTSMS 19; Cambridge: Cambridge University Press, 1972) 61–4.

However, the passages are in closest agreement at precisely the point where our investigation is critical: Luke 22:25–6a. The differences we find here are not the 'result of independent renderings of the same passage,' but the conscious attempt of Luke to show the empire in a favorable light.
123 It is interesting to note that Luke retains the verb δοκῶ, but he moves it from the realm of secular rule and into the midst of the disciples themselves. It is τὸ τίς αὐτῶν δοκεῖ εἶναι μείζων.
124 For the force of these κατά compound words see C. F. D. Moule, *An Idiom Book of the New Testament* (Cambridge: Cambridge University Press, second edition, 1959) 87: 'Prepositions compounded with verbs tend to retain their original adverbial nature.' The normal meaning of κατά with the genitive is 'down, against.' Hence a ruler who not only rules (κυριεύειν) but subdues (κατακυριεύειν) his people, stands over and against them (in a hostile sense).

The Marcan word κατακυριεύουσιν is used in the LXX and almost always conveys the idea of the rule of an alien power: Gen. 1:28; Num. 21:24; Ps. 9:26, 31; 119:133; Dan. 11:39; I Mac. 15:30.

In the New Testament the force of the κατά may clearly be seen in 1 Peter 5:2–3. Also, Luke himself knows the compound verb for he uses it in Acts

19:16: a man having an evil spirit 'leaped on them[who would attempt to exorcize his demon by the name of Jesus], subduing them all he overpowered them' (κατακυριεύσας ἀμφοτέρων ἴσχυσεν κατ' αὐτῶν).

For a contrary viewpoint, one might read R. Cassidy's *Jesus, Politics and Society*. Though Cassidy's interpretation of Luke's presentation of Jesus may have value for our contemporary situation, his research creates more problems than it solves. His redaction criticism, especially with this passage, is not thorough enough. Indeed, his whole notion of Jesus' (and Luke's) 'deference' to political authority rests on Jesus' 'sarcastic' comment about gentile kings and benefactors who 'dominate and subjugate others' (37, 39, 47–48, 60, 74, 130, 150 n.14, 201 n.5). Moreover, Cassidy's presentation of first-century Christian history is not sufficiently careful ('certainly in AD 94 [during the reign of Domitian], Christians were persecuted by Roman emperors'; 5), and placement of Luke in the broader Hellenistic (or even New Testament) literary context is lacking.

125 H. D. Betz notes that Plutarch (*De se ips. cit. invid. laud.* 12) 'approves of those rulers who adopt names which are highly respectable, but still human ... like Philadelphos, Philometor, Euergetès or Theophilès, instead of allowing themselves to be proclaimed "gods" or "sons of gods" ...' (H. D. Betz, *Plutarch's Ethical Writings and Early Christian Literature* [Leiden: Brill, 1978] 374). Cf. A. D. Nock, 'Soter and Euergetes,' 127–48.

The word group εὐεργετῶ, εὐεργέτης, εὐεργεσία is generally avoided by the Greek translators of the Old Testament. Where it does occur the benefactor is (except for Prov. 11:17) always God. In the later Hellenistic Jewish writings a shift is made to include earthly princes, including the emperor, as 'Benefactors'; 2 Mac. 4:2, 3 Mac. 3:19; 6:24; Philo, *Op. Mund.* 169; *Leg. All.* 2.55; *Leg. Gai.* 20, 149; *Vit. Mos.* 2.198; Josephus, *JW* 3.459.

In the New Testament the word group occurs four times, three of these in Luke's writings. In Acts 4:9 it is the apostles who bring 'benefits' (εὐεργεσία) and 'healing/salvation' (σέσωται). Luke makes clear the source of these apostolic benefits in Acts 10:38: 'God anointed Jesus of Nazareth with the Holy Spirit and with power, who went about doing beneficial deeds (εὐεργετῶν) and healing (ἰώμενος) all that were oppressed (καταδυναστευομένους) by the devil.' We should also note that oppression is promoted by the devil while benefits are the gift of God (Acts 19:16).

126 A. Deissmann, *Light from the Ancient East*, tr. by L. Strachan (London: Doran, 1927) 253, Nock, *op. cit.*; Josephus, *JW* 3.459.

127 C. K. Barrett, *Luke the Historian*, 63.

128 See C. H. Talbert, *Literary Patterns*, Chapter 2.

3. The trial of Jesus

1 Paul also puts the blame for Jesus' death on 'the Jews' (1 Thes. 2:14–15), but fails to specify which Jews. Paul Winter, in his excellent study, of the trial of Jesus, has noted that even prior to Luke, Mark 'wishes to emphasize the culpability of the Jewish nation for the death of Jesus, particularly of its leaders; they, not the Romans, are to be held responsible for the crucifixion. It is not to be assumed that the Evangelist was moved by positively anti-Jewish sentiments; his tendency was defensive rather than aggressive. He was concerned to avoid mentioning anything that would provoke Roman antagonism towards, or

even suspicion of, the ideals for which he stood' (*On the Trial of Jesus* [Berlin: De Gruyter, 1961] 24). I would suggest that Luke has taken Mark's perspective one step further; Luke was no longer so concerned about Roman opinion as he was to promote accommodation with the empire.

Richard Cassidy rightly emphasizes that 'the chief priests and their allies' are the villains in Luke's account (*Jesus, Politics, and Society*, 69–70). However, Cassidy's analysis of the trial narrative is much too thin and does not do justice to Luke's political and theological sophistication. He never asks why in Luke's presentation the Sanhedrin asks two questions instead of one (as in Mark) (63–4), nor does he investigate Pilate's strange response to one accused of treason ('... Pilate and Herod discerned almost immediately that Jesus was not a Zealot or comparable to the Zealots ...' [76] – if this be the case then why the *titulus* on the cross?), nor does he note the subtle difference between what actually happened at Golgotha (a *Roman* crucifixion) and the *impression* that Luke is trying to make on the reader (71–2) – that not the Romans, but either the Herodians or the temple guard are responsible for carrying out the crucifixion; see below, pp. 44–5.

2 A posthumous publication of V. Taylor has recently reactivated his thesis that Luke was not dependent on Mark for an outline of the passion narrative; he rather had a special written continuous account into which he spliced details from the Marcan tradition (*The Passion Narrative of St. Luke*). Evans has done an outstanding job of preparing this book for publication by including the latest arguments on both sides of the proto-Luke hypothesis dispute. One notes, however, that at precisely the points where one might see the hand of Luke adjusting his sources to fit his perspective, Taylor also makes similar concessions; cf. esp. 82–4, 86–9. With respect to the two very different questions put to Jesus by the Sanhedrin, Taylor does not notice the distinction which Luke has made: 'When they all *repeat the question*, ... [Jesus] does not deny that he is the Messiah ...' (135, my emphasis).

3 R. S. Rogers, in his study *Criminal Trials and Criminal Legislation under Tiberius* (Middletown, CT: American Philological Association, 1935), notes how strongly political the charges were against Jesus. The charges of fomenting rebellion, forbidding payment of taxes, and claiming sovereignty were too well known for Luke to cover over by stressing the religious dimensions of those charges.

Rogers indicates that under Tiberius there are 106 recorded cases of *maiestas* (24 cases of *lèse majesté*, 82 cases of *perduellio*, which are often difficult to differentiate; 191–4). This represents over half the recorded indictments brought against identified persons; 194. For some reason Rogers sets apart four indictments on the charge of *vis publicus*; 198. I suspect, however, that these also belong under the rubric *maiestas*. Especially in the charges against Jesus, *perduellio* and *vis publicus* are linked together. It is apparent that Luke views the second charge more easily proven and therefore minimizes the importance of the cleansing of the temple (compare Mark 11: 15–19 and John 2:13–17). The *lex Iulia* relating to public and private violence expressly states that 'anyone who, appearing armed in public and in company with armed men, besieges, surrounds, closes, or occupies any temple, gate, or other public property,' is liable under this law for prosecution and punishment (Paulus *Sent.* 5.26.3). The violence in the temple caused by Jesus is not mentioned in the Lucan account of the trial and, unlike Luke's treatment of his sources elsewhere, the actual temple violence is reduced to a whisper. To have reported the extent of Jesus' action as did the other gospels would mean that Jesus' actions would also have to be accounted for in his trial, and under Roman law with regard to public violence Luke knows that Jesus would have been found guilty. Luke, therefore, is forced to ignore the cleansing of the temple in the trial and reduce the scope of its violence in the cleansing scene.

Also see R. S. Rogers, 'Treason in the Early Empire,' *JRS* XLIX (1959) 90–4; C. W. Chilton, 'The Roman Law of Treason under the Early Principate,' *JRS* XLV (1965) 73–81.

4 E.g., W. Manson, *Luke*, 253; E. Klostermann, *Das Lukasevangelium* (HNT 2/1; Tübingen: Mohr, 1929) 588; G. W. H. Lampe, 'Luke,' *Peake's Commentary on the Bible* (London: Nelson, 1962) 733h.

5 Cf. B. S. Easton, *Luke*, 337. The phrase in 22:70 ('Ὑμεῖς λέγετε ὅτι ἐγώ εἰμι) must be distinguished from the statement of Jesus in 23:3 (Σὺ λέγεις). B. H. Streeter thinks that 'the Σὺ εἶπας of Matthew [26:64] and the 'Ὑμεῖς λέγετε of Luke [22:70] are independent adaptations of the Σὺ λέγεις of Mk. XV. 2, intended to assimilate our Lord's reply to the High Priest to His reply to Pilate' (B. H. Streeter, *The Four Gospels* [rev. edition, New York: Macmillan, 1930] 322; cf. E. Klostermann, *Das Lukasevangelium*, 588).

In the latter passage (23:3) Luke followed his source strictly, and he probably understood Jesus' reply as Mark intended it – evasively and rhetorically. The former passage (22:70) however, is not a Lucan adaptation, but a Lucan emphasis of the culpability of the Jews.

On the discussion of the two questions put to Jesus by the Sanhedrin, see F. L. Godet, *Commentary*, II, 318. O. Cullmann sees Jesus (not Luke!) deliberately correcting the high priest's question by substituting 'Son of Man' for 'Messiah' (*The Christology of the New Testament*) [London: SCM, 1959] 120). H. Flender (*St. Luke*, 44, n.5) attempts to correct Cullmann: 'Even those who, unlike Cullmann, do not presume a historical scene, will be able to accept his argument on this passage, but as Lucan theology. Cullmann works out the Lucan theology and then presents it as an account of history.' Flender (p. 45) also states that the οὖν of 22:70 refers to verse 69. More likely it refers not to Jesus' explanation of the Son of Man, but to verse 67, thus bringing back the second half of the Marcan question (14:61b).

6 G. B. Caird (*Luke*, 246) declares that Pilate had 'enough sagacity to see through their [the Sanhedrin's] duplicity ...' That Pilate would have been sage about the various notions of Messiah, including Jesus' own interpretation, is not likely.

7 Deut. 19:15; Num. 35:30; cf. G. F. Moore, *Judaism in the First Centuries of the Christian Era*, II (Cambridge, MA: Harvard University Press, 1927–30) 184–7.

8 Luke 23:2. Luke has already dismissed all three charges against Jesus: (1) Jesus has not perverted the nation; it already was perverse (9:41); (2) Jesus has already specifically charged those sent as spies by the scribes and chief priests to 'render to Caesar his tribute' (20:22, φόρος: note that Luke removes the Latinism of his source [Mark 12:14 reads κῆνσος] as he frequently does: Luke 8:16; 12:59; 23:47); (3) Jesus did not, as we have already noted, accept the messianic title as the Sanhedrin intended it, i.e., politically. We must note, however, that Luke has laid the groundwork for such a possible accusation by having the people acclaim Jesus not only as he 'who comes in the name of the Lord' (Mark 11:10), but as 'the *king* who comes in the name of the Lord' (19:38).

The cry of the people, 'peace in heaven and glory in the highest,' is similar to that given by the shepherds at Jesus' birth, 'peace on earth, good will toward men' (2:14). B. S. Easton (*Luke*, 287) points out that the parallel runs from the preceding verse of each acclamation (2:13–14/19:37–8). Thus Luke echoes the cry of those under the *pax romana*, cf. Virgil, *Eclogues* 4; *Aeneid* 1. 278–96; Tacitus, *Ann.* 1.2; *Hist.* 1.1; Appian, *BC* 5.130; *Res Gestae* 13, 26. Luke has emphasized to his readers that Jesus was indeed a king, though not in the earthly political sense (cf. H. Flender, *St. Luke*, 61). As he was hailed by the angels from heaven at his birth, so now at his fateful entry into Jerusalem he is hailed by the people on earth.

Three similar charges were also laid against Paul and Silas by the Jews of Thessalonica: (1) 'These men have turned the world upside down (τὴν οἰκουμένην ἀναστατώσαντες) ...; (2) they are acting against the decrees of Caesar (τῶν δογμάτων Καίσαρος); (3) they say that there is another king (βασιλέα ἕτερον), Jesus' (Acts 17:6b–7).

9 Luke 23:5. There is no doubt that such accusations as were laid against Jesus were becoming increasingly common in the civil court of Jerusalem before the fall of that city; cf. Josephus, *JW* 1.5; 2.55–65, 258–65, 403–7, 433–4. Tacitus, *Hist.* 5.9: 'After Herod's death, a certain Simon assumed the name of king without awaiting for Caesar's decision. He, however, was put to death by Quintilius Varus, governor of Syria.'

One notes in Josephus a lack of references to court dealings with messianic pretenders, and in the case just mentioned (Simon) he gives information which contradicts Tacitus. While Tacitus claims that Simon was executed, Josephus maintains that Simon was intercepted in battle by Gratus, commander of the royal infantry, who struck off his head with the sword. This seems not atypical of the way political messiahs met their end in Josephus' writings. See also S. G. F. Brandon, *Zealots*, 32–4, 52–4.

10 A. N. Sherwin-White, *Roman Society*, 65.

11 The *locus classicus* is Pliny's handling of Romans suspected of participating in Christian practices in Pontus (*Epistle* 10.96). One may also cite the edict of Tiberius on appeals of criminal (and in particular capital) cases which, if too difficult to handle at the local level, the litigant (the Sanhedrin) might appeal or the trial judge might remit to the emperor (S. Riccobono, *Fontes iuris romani antejustiniani* [Florence: Barbera, 1940] 452–4). We only note these examples with caution, however, because they deal primarily with accused Roman citizens, which Jesus was not. Though it was not mandatory to do so in Jesus' case, Pilate, if he desired, could have consulted Rome about the trial; cf. *Dig.* 47.23.2.

12 Sherwin-White, *Roman Society*, 13–15; A. H. M. Jones, 'I Appeal unto Caesar,' *Studies in Roman Government and Law*, 53–65.

13 J. Blinzler, *The Trial of Jesus*, tr. by I. and F. McHugh (Westminster, MD: Newman, 1959) 177–84; A. H. M. Jones, *The Herods of Judaea* (Oxford: Clarendon Press, 1938) 172–74; E. Schürer, *History of the Jewish People*, I, 383–87; P. Winter, *Trial*, 51–61. Blinzler rather nicely lays out the situation between the Jews and Pilate in the trial of Jesus: 'Because he despised the Jews and eagerly availed himself of every opportunity of letting them see it, he inevitably adopted an attitude of opposition when he received the strange and unreasonable request to condemn and execute without more ado the prisoner

they brought before him. His resistance and mistrust inevitably increased when he ascertained that the accused was to be sent to His death on account of a political offense, of all things! So the representatives of this obstreperous and rebellious race were trying to persuade him that they were acting purely out of loyalty to Rome! It did not require any particular sagacity on Pilate's part to realize that some quite different motives must lie behind the Sanhedrin's demand. They wanted to get rid of someone who had become obnoxious to them, and he, the Roman official, was to serve as their tool in this. Seen in this light, the resistance of Pilate to the Jews' demand is completely understandable' (183). One aspect, however, that Blinzler and others disregard in dealing with the trial of Jesus is the connection between Rome and the high priest. The high priest was an appointee of Rome and his loyalty was expected and received; in Jesus' time, the high priest and his party formed the backbone of the conservative element which remained loyal to the Roman government. It is doubtful that even out of spite Pilate would have ignored the charges of that party, especially if he had any idea that they might have appealed directly to Rome. The mode of Jesus' death, of course, attests to the fact that he did believe their charges.

14 Winter, *Trial*, 50.

15 Luke 9:22; 17:25; 22:37; 24:7, 26, 44–6. See δεῖ, βουλή, and θέλημα in Matthew, Mark, and Acts.

16 Bultmann, *History*, 282; see the list in H. Conzelmann, *Luke*, 137, n.1.

17 F. J. Godet, *Commentary*, II, 321; A. Plummer, *Luke*, 522.

18 Sherwin-White, *Roman Society*, 31, n.5; H. W. Hoehner, *Herod Antipas* (SNTSMS 17; Cambridge: Cambridge University, 1972) 239.

19 G. B. Caird, *Gospel of Luke*, 247; J. A. Findlay, 'Luke,' *Abingdon Bible Commentary* (New York: Abingdon, 1929) 1056; cf. Luke 8:3; Acts 13:1.

20 T. Mommsen, *Römisches Strafrecht*, 356–7.

21 Sherwin-White, *Roman Society*, 31; cf. Josephus, *JW* 1.474.

22 M. Dibelius, *From Tradition to Gospel* tr. by B. L. Woolf (New York: Scribner's, 1935) 199; 'Herodes und Pilatus,' *ZNTW* XVI (1915) 113–26; H. J. Cadbury, *MLA*, 231. R. Bultmann (*History*, 273) considers that the account was created by a predecessor.

23 In 9:7, Luke corrects the title given to Herod by Mark (6:14), and in Acts 12:1 he rightly refers to 'Herod [Agrippa] the king.'

24 H. J. Cadbury, *MLA*, 310; J. Munck, *The Acts of the Apostles* (AB, 31; Garden City, NY: Doubleday, 1967) lxxvii–lxxviii; H. Flender, *Luke*, 131; cf. H. Conzelmann, *Luke*, 217, n.2.

25 Creed, *Gospel According to Luke*, 280. We also note that the temple guard who arrested Jesus also mocked and beat him (Luke 22:52, 63–5).

26 H. Conzelmann, *Luke*, 86–8, esp. 88 n.1.

27 Mark elsewhere uses the Greek term μαστιγῶ (Mark 10:34/Luke 18:33). Cf. also Josephus, *JW* 2.306; 5.449; 7.200–2, where rebels are first scourged (μαστιγῶ) and then crucified.

28 A. N. Sherwin-White, on the basis of *Dig.* 28.19.7, suggests that there were three grades of beatings in the empire: *fustes, flagella, verbera* (p. 27). However, neither the New Testament nor the Roman legal sources are clear in distinguishing the function or severity of the last two cases. The first was obviously the lightest, but the last two were both severe whippings. We should also note that

beating was meted out for three reasons (which do not always correspond with the three types of beating): (1) as a warning to a potential trouble-maker, which was done with rods and is probably what Luke had in mind in 23:16, 22, (cf. Acts 16:22; Strabo, *Geog.* 5.2.; Epictetus, *Diss.* 4.1.57; 4.1.20−1; Paulus, *Sent.* 5.2.1; *Dig.* 48.2.6; 48.19.28; Josephus, *JW* 2.269); (2) as a means of obtaining a confession (Acts 22:24−5; Josephus, *JW* 6.304; *Dig.* 3.7.32; Paulus, *Sent.* 5.26.1; 5.28.2); (3) and as a prelude to crucifixion, an intrinsic part of the capital sentence (Josephus, *JW* 2.306; 5.449; 7.200−2; Cicero, *In Verr.* 5.64; *In Phil.* 66; Tacitus, *Hist.* 5.3.11).

J. Blinzler (*The Trial*, 222−6, 233−5) also presents a thorough discussion of Roman scourging. From the evidence of the sources, however, Blinzler appears mistaken on several points: (1) That scourging was in itself a death sentence. Not only was this not the case, but Blinzler even says that the 'death sentence' was carried out by *fustuarium*, which, as we noted, was the lightest of the beatings. (2) That Pilate ordered the scourging as an 'independent punishment.' This is Blinzler's interpretation of both Luke and John (19:4). But the Lucan passage gives the impression that the beating was meant to be a warning, while the Johannine setting seems to indicate that Pilate's motive for scourging was the extraction of a confession. Neither was a punishment resulting from a sentence. (3) That the scourging was not 'a *subsidiary* punishment preceding execution.' At this point Blinzler confuses the synoptic accounts, which are quite different, as their vocabulary and sequence indicate. Mark and Matthew bring out quite clearly what has been noted in other sources, that scourging preceded crucifixion as part and parcel of the punishment.

29 Plummer, *Gospel According to Luke*, 525; cf. G. Bertram, *TDNT*, V (1967) 621, n.160.

30 Luke's omission of the Marcan reference to the Roman mocking and scourging does not mean that he was unaware of that incident. In the third prediction of the passion, Luke closely followed his source (Mark 10:33−4/Luke 18:32−3). There are two issues which must be raised when comparing these two passages: (1) Why did Luke omit 'the Son of Man will be delivered to the chief priests and scribes, and they will condemn him to death (κατακρινοῦσιν αὐτὸν θανάτῳ), and deliver him to the Gentiles'? I believe he made this omission because he did not consider the Sanhedrin to constitute legitimate authority, especially over capital offenses against the state. They cannot condemn, but only bring charges. (2) By changing Mark's future active verbs to future passive verbs, Luke has made doubtful in the minds of his readers the complicity of the Gentiles in the shameful treatment of Jesus (ἐμπαίξουσιν becomes ἐμπαιχθήσεται; ἐμπτύσουσιν becomes ἐμπτυσθήσεται). Luke cannot sustain this fiction, however, for the scourging and crucifixion are presented substantially the same as in his source: μαστιγώσαντες ἀποκτενοῦσιν αὐτόν. Luke knew these important details of Jesus' trial and yet he suppressed them in his trial narrative.

31 Both groups of police would have been composed of Jews, though Herod's officers may have been Roman (as I think Luke indicates in 23:47); cf. pp. 32−4.

32 Luke's military vocabulary does not clearly indicate which soldiers report to Jewish authorities and which are under the *imperium*.

33 Cf. G. D. Kilpatrick, 'A Theme of the Lucan Passion Story and Luke xxiii, 47,'

JTS XLIII (1942) 35–6. V. Taylor concluded that Luke's account of the centurion's confession is not based on Mark 15:39, but is his use of δίκαιος a modification of Mark's υ ἱὸς θεοῦ (*Passion Narrative*, 96). However, position, percentage of identical words, and a typical Lucan improvement of Mark's Latinism (κεντυρίων becomes ἑκατοντάρχης) make it very difficult to accept Taylor's conclusion with regard to this passage.

34 Cf. *MLA*, 245–9. Luke 2:22, 41–5; 5:17; 6:17; 13:22; 17:11; 18:31; 19:11, 28.

35 Luke 24:46–52.

36 We might also include 13:34–5 which is a Q saying introduced by a piece of Lucan theology: 'It cannot be that a prophet should perish away from Jerusalem' (32). It will probably be more advantageous and to the point of this study to stay with what appears to be Luke's own material.
 One other prophetic oracle which has been badly sliced up and misplaced is 9:51, 53a. Since it is impossible to know whether the butchering was done by Luke or a clumsy scribe we must also exclude this passage from consideration here.

37 Flender, 18, cf. 17, 108.

38 H. Chadwick, 'The Circle and the Ellipse,' 25.

39 L. Gaston, *No Stone on Another* (Leiden: Brill, 1970) 370–487.

40 Certainly the church would have come to recognize Rome as the political center; by the time of Clement of Rome, the imperial capital may also have become the Christian religious center.

41 2 Sam. 7:13; 1 Ki. 8:10–19, 27–30; 9:3; Ps. 46, 74; Isa. 6:1–5; Jer. 25:30; Joel 3:16; Amos 1:2. Also in Isa. 8:18: 'I (Isaiah) and the children whom the Lord has given me are signs and portents (σημεῖα καὶ τέρατα) in Israel from the Lord of hosts, who dwells on Mount Zion.' Cf. Acts 2:22, 43; 4:30; 5:13; etc.

42 'Name' – Acts 2:21, 38; 4:7, 10, 12, 17–18, 30 (in Jerusalem)
 8:12–13 (in Samaria)
 9:15–16, 27 (in Damascus)
 10:48 (in Caesarea)
 16:18 (in Philippi)
 19:5 (in Ephesus)
Most of these citations refer to the name of Jesus and concur with an early Christian theological understanding that the name of Jesus had an exalted status with the power to bring about salvation and to produce miracles (Phil. 2:9–11; Rom. 10:9; Eph. 1:20–21). This theme of the exalted name of Jesus is clearly presented by Luke in Acts 4:7–12. Paul (Rom. 10:13) and Luke (Acts 2:21) refer to Joel 2:32 as a supporting text.
'Word' – Acts 4:4, 29, 31 (Jerusalem)
 8:4, 14, 25 (Samaria)
 10:44; 11:1 (Caesarea)
 13:5 (Salamis)
 14:3 (Iconium)
 14:25 (Perga)
 15:35 (Antioch)
'Glory' – In Acts 7:55 the 'glory of God' shines forth from heaven and Jesus 'stands' in judgment over Jerusalem (Cf. R. Pesch, 'Die Vision des Stephanus Apg. 7, 55ff., im Rahmen der Apostelgeschichte,' *Bib.*

Leben IX [2, 1965] 92–107, [3, 1965] 170–83. Cf. also As. Mos.
10.3; Isa. 3:13 [LXX] where the magistrate stands to pronounce
judgment). After the judgment the church is 'scattered.' Also in all
three accounts of the Christophany, Paul sees the glorious bright light
on the road to Damascus (Acts 22:11; cf. 9:3; 26:13) and is commissioned in that light to preach the gospel to the nations.

43 Acts 8:1, 4; 17:24. Similarly Josephus and Tacitus record a tradition that before
the fall of Jerusalem 'a voice as of a host' cried out, 'We are departing hence.'
(Josephus, *JW* 6.300: μετὰ δὲ ταῦτα φωνῆς ἀθρόας, μεταβαίνομεν ἐντεῦθεν.
Tacitus, *Hist.* 5.13: *et audita maior humana vox excedere deos.*) Josephus also
claims that the Zealots had already profaned the Temple by murdering the chief
priests. '... God had, for its pollutions, condemned the city to destruction and
desired to purge the sanctuary by fire ...' (*JW* 4.323; cf. 5.19.) '... God himself,
for loathing of their [the Zealots'] impiety, turned away from our city and,
because He deemed the Temple to be no longer a clean dwelling place for Him,
brought the Romans upon us and purification by fire upon the city ...' (*Ant.*
20.166)
    The Rabbis also transmit a tradition that with the approach of the Roman
army the Shekinah had left Jerusalem and journeyed to dwell among the
diaspora: M. Rab. Lam. 1.33, 54; Yoma 56b (Cf. R. T. Herford, *Christianity in
Talmud and Midrash* [Clifton, NJ: Reference Book Publishers, 1903, reprinted
1966], 247ff.); also Syr. Bar. 8.2. Cf. B. Gärtner, *The Temple and the Community in Qumran and the New Testament* (SNTSMS 1; Cambridge: Cambridge
University Press, 1965) 57–8, 116.

44 V. Taylor, *Behind the Third Gospel*, 109–25; T. W. Manson, *The Sayings of
Jesus as Recorded in the Gospels of St. Matthew and St. Luke* (London: SCM,
1954), 319–22, 328–31, 342–3; C. H. Dodd, 'The Fall of Jerusalem and the
"Abomination of Desolation,"' *More New Testament Studies* (Grand Rapids,
MI: Eerdmans, 1968), 69–83; H. Conzelmann, *Theology of St. Luke*, 125–
36; W. Marxsen, *Mark the Evangelist* (Nashville, TN: Abingdon, 1969), 151–
206 (especially 190–8); H. Flender, *St. Luke*, 17–18, 107–17. One should
also include the American, William C. Robinson, whose Basel dissertation
certainly reflects the German position; *The Way of the Lord*, 78–86, 90–2.

45 Cadbury, *MLA*, 219, 222–9, 242. Even if Luke uses older oracular tradition
concerning the fate of the Holy City, he retains the Semitic flavoring and
puts it into the mouth of Jesus; Conzelmann, *Theology of St. Luke*, 125.

46 Flender, *St. Luke*, 108. The passion 'is framed by two scenes which point to
the impending judgment upon the Jews. One is the scene of Jesus weeping over
the city (19:41–4) and the other is the people weeping for Jesus (23:27–31).'

47 Conzelmann, *Theology of St. Luke*, 134, n.1.

48 Tacitus, *Hist.* 2.4, 5.4; cf. 1.10; 5.5, 13: Suetonius, *Vesp.* 4.

49 Tacitus, *Hist.* 5.11.

4. The trial of Paul

1 The vitality of the Tübingen school has survived, but not always the balance.
Martin Dibelius and his disciples put emphasis on Paul the Roman. His essays
on Acts laid the foundation for Lucan research in the latter half of this century
(*Studies in the Acts of the Apostles*). According to Dibelius Luke wrote a

political defense of Christianity in Acts 21–8 using Paul as a cipher for the politically harmless sect.

'So within the framework of Paul's trial, Luke presents Christian belief with an apologetic purpose, and it is only because of this purpose that his description of the trial is so elaborate' (213).

While rejecting Dibelius' revival of the political aspect of the Tübingen hypothesis, Jacob Jervell has resurrected the irenic motif; *Luke and the People of God* (Minneapolis: Augsburg, 1972). In a sophisticated argument, Jervell concludes that the speeches of Paul were not intended as a political defense of the apostle or the church. Rather, 'the issue is the justification of the church's existence, and indirectly concern for the Gentile mission' (173). By means of the apologetic speeches Luke has attempted to combat rumors about Paul (was he an apostate from Judaism?) and to commend the apostle (and the gentile mission) to the Jewish Christians (175–7).

2 Luke 12:11; 21:14; Acts 19:33; 22:1; 24:10; 25:8, 16; 26:1, 2, 24.

3 Rom. 2:15; 1 Cor. 9:3; 2 Cor. 7:11; 12:19; Phil. 1:7, 16; 2 Tim. 4:16; 1 Pet. 3:15.

4 The appearance of 'apology' in the non-Pauline, non-Lucan New Testament literature is also illuminating. 1 Pet. 3:15 recommends, unlike Luke's Gospel (21:14), that the believer should 'always be prepared to make a defense to anyone who asks you about the hope which you have.' While it is not clear that the author has a legal context in mind, the *content* of the defense is the Christian 'hope,' the resurrection (1:3, 21).

The author of 2 Tim. 4:16 suggests that at his 'first defense' Paul was able fully to proclaim the kerygma; S. G. Wilson, *Luke and the Pastoral Epistles*, 40. This perspective fits rather well with what we know of Paul's hearings before Felix, Festus, and Agrippa.

5 For an excellent summary of the argumentation about the letter's place of composition, see R. P. Martin, *Philippians* (NCB; London: Oliphants 1976) 36–57. I do not intend, in this short excursus on Philippians, to review the vast discussion related to such items as date, place of composition, or integrity of the letter. The diversity of opinion on any of these items, not to mention a definitive resolution of them, is sufficient to drive one to despair.

I see no overwhelming difficulty in accepting the traditional provenance of this letter, Rome, c. A.D. 60–2, for which B. Reicke has made a convincing case ('Caesarea, Rome, and the Captivity Epistles,' *Apostolic History and the Gospel*, ed. by W. Gasque and R. P. Martin (Grand Rapids, MI: Eerdmans, 1970) 277–86; cf. F. W. Beare, *The Epistle to the Philippians* [HNTC; New York: Harper, 1959] 15–24). This 'older' solution has in its favor both internal (the 'praetorian guard' and 'Caesar's household' are mentioned) and external (Paul's two-year Roman imprisonment mentioned in Acts 28) support. Paul's confinement is a serious matter which could lead to life or death for the apostle (1:19–24, 29–30; 2:17). That his account does not tally with the comparative freedom expressed in Acts 28 is not surprising in light of Luke's pro-Roman perspective. It could also be that Paul's letter reflects changed circumstances from 'free custody' to a strict confinement.

It should be noted, however, that there are several problems with this solution. (a) The letter presupposes at least two, and perhaps as many as five, journeys between Paul's place of confinement and Philippi (from Rome, 800

miles; from Caesarea, 1200 miles; from Ephesus or Corinth, about 200 miles).
Two years' time (Acts 28), while sufficient for two journeys, may not have been
enough for five trips to and from Rome (Deissmann, 'Zur ephesinischen Gefangenschaft des Apostels Paulus,' *Anatolian Studies Presented to Sir W. M. Ramsay*,
ed. by W. H. Buckler and W. M. Calder [Manchester: Manchester University
Press, 1923] 121–7). P. N. Harrison, C. H. Dodd, and B. Reicke see no difficulty
in fitting in as many as five trips in two years' time (Harrison, 'The Pastoral
Epistles and Duncan's Ephesian Theory,' *NTS* II [1965–6] 260; Dodd, 'The
Mind of Paul,' *New Testament Studies* [New York: Scribner's, 1953] 96–9;
cf. G. S. Duncan, *St Paul's Ephesian Ministry* [New York: Scribner's, 1930]).
(b) Paul expresses the hope of revisiting Philippi should his release be granted.
In Paul's earlier letter to the Roman church, the implication is that his work in
the East is complete and his desire is to begin new missionary work in the West
(Rom. 15:23, 24, 28). This objection does not allow for Paul, out of gratitude
to the Philippian church, to revise his plans during his long ordeal in the courts.
(c) Luke is not mentioned, as we might expect from the 'we' passage in Acts
27–8, in Philippians. This argument from silence proves nothing.

The only other reasonable candidates for the provenance of Philippians are
Caesarea, AD 58 (W. Michaelis, *Die Datierung des Philipperbriefs* [Gütersloh:
Bertelsmann, 1933] : E. Lohmeyer, *Der Brief an die Philipper* [KEK; Göttingen:
Vandenhoeck & Ruprecht, 1929, reprinted 1974]), and Ephesus, AD 53–5
(Deissmann, *Light from the Ancient East*; Duncan, *Ephesian Ministry*; J. H.
Michael, *The Epistle of Paul to the Philippians* (MNTC; New York: Harper,
1928), with Ephesus having the edge over Caesarea. The major difficulties with
Caesarea are (a) the custody of Acts 23–4 does not reflect the desperate situation
of imminent martyrdom suggested in Phil. 1:20–4; 2:17, and (b) the size and
type of Christian community alluded to in Phil. 1:14–17 suggests a large center
(not likely Caesarea) where Christian diversity and presence is being felt.

The case for Ephesus relies heavily on inferences drawn from Paul's letters.
In 1 Cor. 15:32 Paul recalls that at Ephesus he contended with 'wild beasts.'
Furthermore, Paul states that he was in bonds several times (2 Cor. 11:23–7;
cf. 1 Clem. 5.6), and had so devastating an experience in Asia that, despairing
of life, 'we felt that we had received the sentence of death' (2 Cor. 1:8–9).

M. Dibelius' conclusion states well the frustrating impasse scholars have
reached in assigning a place of origin for Philippians: 'therefore a definite
solution of this problem can hardly be reached because, even if we consider it
difficult to imagine its having been composed at Rome, the Ephesian hypothesis still rests on mere supposition'; *An die Thessalonicher I, II, An die Philipper*
(HNT; Tübingen: Mohr, 1937) 98.

The abrupt caesura at Phil. 3:1 indicates to many scholars an interpolated
section, 3:1b–21 (Michael; Beare; J. Gnilka, *Die Philipperbrief* [HThKNT;
Freiburg: Herder, 1968]). R. Jewett and T. E. Pollard, however, have demonstrated the literary interconnections between chapter 3 and the rest of the
letter; in particular, note the Greek root πολιτ - found only in 1:27 and 3:20
in the letters of Paul (Jewett, 'The Epistolary Thanksgiving and the Integrity
of Philippians,' *NovT* XII [1970] 40–53; Pollard, 'The Integrity of Philippians,'
NTS XIII [1966–7] 57–66). Furthermore, it is difficult to say with certainty
that Paul has in mind two different sets of 'enemies of the cross' in Chapters 1
and 2 (W. Schmithals, *Paul and the Gnostics*, tr. by J. E. Steely [Nashville:

Abingdon, 1972] 65–122). It may simply be that Paul was only warming up, as it were, in 1:28, and then moves in to flay these opponents in 3:19. In the final analysis, the issue of an interpolation is not terribly important, for the whole of the letter – whether or not it was stitched together – reflects Paul's outlook as he awaits trial.

6 Beare, *Epistle*, 53; M. R. Vincent, *A Critical and Exegetical Commentary on the Epistles to the Philippians and to Philemon* (ICC; Edinburgh: T. & T. Clark, 1897, reprinted 1961) 9–10. Also see 1 Cor. 1:6–8 where βεβαιῶ is linked with μαρτύριον and ἀνέγκλητος (though the context is theological, the terms are drawn from the courtroom; cf. Heb. 6:16).

7 It may be, as some commentators have suggested (see note 5), that Chapter 3 is an interpolated fragment of another Pauline letter (possibly also sent to Philippi). In this chapter Paul is warning against those who would impose circumcision upon gentile Christians. Imbedded here, however, is a continuation of the apologetic theme of Chapter 1: Paul's righteousness is not based on law, either Jewish or Roman, but on faith in Christ. This sums up Paul's position with respect to his adversaries who proclaim that he has abrogated his Pharisaic heritage.

8 C. H. Dodd has suggested that Paul's gospel may be identified with the recounting of Jesus' life, death, and resurrection. According to Dodd, the opening verses of 1 Cor. 15 provide a cardinal Pauline kerygmatic statement (*The Apostolic Preaching and Its Developments* [London: Hodder and Stoughton, 1936]; cf. E. P. Sanders, *Paul and Palestinian Judaism* [Philadelphia: Fortress, 1977] 144).

9 J. Knox ('Acts and the Pauline Letter Corpus,' *SLA*, 283–4) declares that the argument about whether or not Luke used Paul's letters is at a stalemate:

> Scholars on the one side, observing that Luke made little or no use of the letters and nowhere refers to Paul as writing them, conclude that he could not have known them; scholars on the other side, sure that Luke could not have failed to know them, conclude that despite the meagerness of actual evidence he must have used them. This impasse should lead us to examine the major premise of both sides, namely: If Luke knew the letters of Paul, he must have used them. I believe we are forced by the literary evidence (or, rather, by the lack of it), on the one hand, and by the a priori probabilities, on the other to question this premise and to consider seriously the possibility that Luke knew, or at least knew of, letters of Paul – even *the* (collected) letters of Paul – and quite consciously and deliberately made little or no use of them.

Luke, according to Knox, is silent about Paul's letters because they are being used (inappropriately) by Marcionite Christians. Luke, therefore, can record the story of Paul, but not his letters.

M. Enslin, spurred by Knox's article, revived his own earlier argument that Luke's silence about Paul's letters does not necessarily mean he did not make use of them ('"Luke" and Paul,' *JAOS* LVIII [1938] 81ff; 'Once Again, Luke and Paul,' *ZNTW* LXI [1970] 253ff.; also see C. K. Barrett, 'The Acts – of Paul,' *New Testament Essays*, 94–5). In addition to the Pauline themes and phrases that Knox finds in Luke–Acts one could also point to a significant correspondence between some of the vocabulary of Philippians and Luke–Acts, particularly the last half of Acts.

(a) πολιτ - is a Greek root occurring in the New Testament only in Luke–Acts (Luke 15:15; 19:14; Acts 21:39; 22:28; 23:1), Philippians (1:27; 3:20), and Ephesians (2:12).

(b) δεσμός in the masculine plural (rather than neuter) is Paul's word for 'chains' (Phil. 1:7, 13, 14, 16; Phm. 10, 13) and also the form used most often by Luke in describing Paul's chains (Acts 22:30; 23:29; 26:29, 31; δεσμά: 20:23; ἄλυσις: 21:33; 28:20).

(c) καταγγέλλω is found only in Acts (10 times, almost exclusively related to the preaching of Paul) and the Pauline letters (6 times, including Phil. 1:16, 18).

(d) ἀφόβως (Phil. 1:14) and ἀκωλύτως (Acts 28:31) point to a similar context in which the apostle was free, even in prison, to communicate his message.

10 The debate over Luke's relationship with Paul has swirled into a blur (see A. J. Mattill, 'The Value of Acts as a Source for the Study of Paul,' *PLA*, 76–98). The 'renewed case against tradition' (Baur's hypothesis representing the old case against tradition: Paul's theology in Acts was mediated by Luke to fit a second-century ecclesiastical need) was fueled by the Bultmann school and ignited by Ph. Vielhauer ('On the Paulinism of Acts,' *SLA*, 33–50; cf. E. Haenchen, *Acts*, 112–16; 'The Book of Acts as Source Material for Early Christianity,' *SLA*, 258–78). The argument is predicated on a fivefold difference between Paul and the author of Acts:

(a) natural theology: the Areopagus speech (Acts 17), developed from Greek philosophy, reflects a positive evaluation of pagan religion (*contra*, Rom. 1:21).

(b) the Law (Baur *redivivus*): there is an absence in Acts of Paul's strong message of freedom from the Law.

(c) Christology: especially missing in Acts is Paul's theology of the cross and the pre-existence of Christ.

(d) eschatology: Luke's salvation history is far removed from the apocalyptic message of Jesus and its Pauline existentialist interpretation.

(e) the person of Paul: in Acts Paul is a miracle-worker and great orator, hardly the Paul of the epistles.

Of course there is also a renewed effort supporting tradition building on Harnack. The critics suppose that Luke, a companion of Paul, 'must thoroughly understand St Paul, he must be of congenial disposition and free from prejudice, he must be absolutely trustworthy and his memory must never fail' (A. Harnack, *Luke the Physician*, tr. by J. R. Wilkinson [London: Williams and Norgate, 1907] 122). Luke, Harnack concluded, was not a disciple of Paul, but his companion. Aside from the positive evidence of a general confluence of events and persons mentioned in Paul's letters and Acts, and the peculiarities of the 'we' sections, the five points listed above may be turned around to provide added evidence that Luke's knowledge of Paul was closer than second-hand.

(a) Gärtner convincingly concludes that the conceptual background of the Areopagus speech is largely Jewish and at no point 'clashes with what is otherwise known of Paul's theology' (*The Areopagus Speech and Natural*

Revelation, tr. by C. H. King [ASNU 21; Uppsala: C. W. K. Gleerup, 1955] 249).

(b) It is not at all clear that Paul was an antinomian, as Vielhauer insists. There is not a shred of evidence that Paul ever taught Jewish Christians to abandon the law. Paul was not anti-law (OT customs and practices) but antilegalism (law as a means of salvation).

(c) Luke's emphasis on the resurrection rather than the cross reflects Paul's own notion that the resurrection is the content of the gospel (1 Cor. 15:2ff.). Furthermore, the Christology of Acts appears to be neither Paul's, nor Luke's, but that of the early church.

(d) For Paul and for Luke it is not the time of the parousia that is important (1 Th. 5:1ff.; Luke 18:8; Acts 1:6–7), but its certainty and suddenness.

(e) With respect to the person of Paul his own letters refer to his miraculous powers (Rom. 15:18–19; 1 Cor. 5:4–5; 2 Cor. 4:7; 12:9, 12; 13:4; 1 Th. 1:5). Finally, he is anything but a 'great orator' in Acts. The Athenians are unmoved, Eutychus falls asleep, and Festus dismisses Paul as mad.

Those who support the traditional view are eventually led to conclude with Harnack that Luke was not a dogged disciple of Paul, but his compassionate companion. According to Ellis, 'Luke's theological independence actually favors the view that he was the Apostle's co-worker and his contemporary, as indeed he claims to be' (*The Gospel of Luke*, 51).

11 Conzelmann, *Luke*, 141–2.

12 Conzelmann, *Luke*, 144. Cf. H. Conzelmann, *Die Apostelgeschichte*, 10; also see Conzelmann's review of Haenchen in *TLZ* LXXXV (1960) 244–5.

13 Conzelmann, *Luke*, 142, my emphasis.

14 K. Löning, *Die Saulustradition in der Apostelgeschichte* (Münster: Verlag Aschendorff, 1973) 186–7.

15 Dibelius in his essay 'Paul in the Acts of the Apostles,' *Studies*, 207–14, claims for Paul *five* hearings. Hearing number three, which I have chosen not to discuss, has little by way of apology and adds virtually nothing to our investigation (Acts 24:24–5; Paul before Felix and Drusilla).

16 H. Cadbury, 'Roman Law,' *BC* V, 302–4 claims that the Sanhedrin scene (with Lysias) was not a trial but a hearing to get information. Yet it is difficult to tell when the 'hearings' cease and the 'trial' begins.

17 Paulus, *Sent.* 5.21.2 (*Qui noues sectas uel ratione incognitas religiones inducent*). While the Roman legal opinions cited in this chapter do come from lists compiled two to three centuries after the writings of Luke, they do, like most written traditions of the period, reflect a legal history that in all probability extends back into the first century. On this problem Sherwin-White notes that 'the precise legal situation of Roman citizens in provincial jurisdiction is not well documented at this period' (*Roman Society*, 57). However, Luke seems not to be a lawyer interested in the legal details of the Pauline trial as much as he is an educated layman presenting in layman's terms his acquaintance with major imperial laws. Luke knows enough to reconstruct in his own way the charges against Paul, charges which are general enough for him to report and not so irregular as to lead the Roman court to make 'landmark decisions.'

18 Josephus, *JW* 5.194; 6.124–5. This report of the Jewish historian was confirmed in 1871 with the discovery of one such slab by M. Clermont-Ganneau which reads: 'No man of another nation may enter within the fence and enclosure

around the temple. And whoever is caught will have himself to blame for his death that ensues.' Cf. Thackeray's *Josephus, The Jewish War*, III, 258–9, n.c., for the Greek text.

19 H. J. Cadbury, 'Roman Law and the Trial of Paul,' *BC*, V, 301.

20 Acts 21:29.

21 Sherwin-White translates the passage: This person was 'stirring up a plague and disturbances for the Jews throughout the world.' From this Sherwin-White concludes that 'Acts is using contemporary language. The charge was precisely the one to bring against a Jew during the principate of Claudius or in the early years of Nero' (*Roman Society*, 51). This is, of course, possible, but too much weight is being placed on one phrase from Claudius' letter to the Alexandrians. Also the charge in Acts is being made by Jews against a fellow Jew, and not by a gentile against Jews. Furthermore we note that in Claudius' letter the word νόσος is used; in Acts, λοιμός. In Sherwin-White's favor, however, we could point to Tacitus' peculiar description of the Christian movement: '... the pernicious superstition was checked for a moment, only to break out again not only in Judea, the source of the disease (*originem eius mali*), but in the capital itself, where all things horrible or shameful in the world collect and find a vogue.' (*Ann.* 15.44)

22 The charge against Paul has been expanded when compared with a charge brought against Jesus. The charge against Jesus was limited to Palestine; the charge against Paul involves the whole of the empire.

23 According to F. J. Cramer, *Astrology in Roman Law and Politics* (Philadelphia: American Philosophical Society, 1954), it was not uncommon to 'throw in for good measure a *maiestas* charge along with other less deadly accusations like adultery, unchastity, or corruption' (252).

24 Cadbury, 'Roman Law,' *BC*, V, 304, n.2.

25 Lake and Cadbury, *BC*, IV, 299.

26 S. P. Scott, *The Civil Law*, XI (New York: AMS Press, 1973) 28, n. i.

27 Paulus, *Sent.* 5.22.1 (*auctores seditionis et tumultus uel concitatores populi ... in insulam deportantur*); cf. *Twelve Tables*, IX; Paulus, *Sent.* 5.29 (*lege Iulia maiestatis*); *Dig.* 48.4.1, 3, 7; and Luke 23:5.

28 Paulus, *Sent.* 5.23.16 (*qui ... fanum templumue, polluerint*).

29 Acts 22:27–8.

30 Acts 24:13.

31 Acts 24:18; cf. 21:24, 26.

32 It is not difficult to see the spirit of Seneca's high ideals (*De Clementia*) as a backdrop against which Luke presents his history of the early church; cf. J. N. Sevenster, *Paul and Seneca* (Leiden: Brill, 1961), and Dibelius, *SLA*, 53–4.

33 Tacitus, *Hist.* 5.9. See Haenchen, *Acts*, 662–3 and Bruce, *Acts*, 421, 427.

34 Acts 25:8. Haenchen, *Acts*, 666, is wrong in holding this verse to be the first indication that a charge of *maiestas* was brought against Paul; cf. Acts 24:5.

35 Haenchen, *Acts*, 669.

36 Or it may well be that by presenting such a *grande finale* to the trials of Paul on Palestinian soil Luke intends to convey that this in fact *was* Paul's last hearing. Since Luke cannot report of such a glorious event at Rome (because Paul's case never came to trial, or because the trial went badly for Paul, or because Paul had died prior to his trial in Rome), this scene at Caesarea must suffice. Cf. H. Cadbury, 'Roman Law,' *BC*, V, 330–1.

37 One normally assumes that Luke was inspired in his description of Paul's trial by the trial of Jesus. However, it may be possible to see the influence working the other way around. This is especially true of Luke's presentation of Herodian involvement in both trials. The detail and content of the Herodian episode in Acts would suggest that Luke is reporting more recent and reliable information than comes through in the Gospel account. Since Paul was brought before both Romans and Herodians then, Luke must have pondered, could one claim less for Jesus? Cf. Cadbury, *MLA*, 310; Munck, *Acts*, lxxvii–lxxviii.

38 Acts 23:29; 25:25; 26:31. In each case Luke uses the formula: $\mu\eta\delta\grave{\epsilon}\nu$ ... $\ddot{\alpha}\xi\iota o\nu$ ... $\theta\alpha\nu\acute{\alpha}\tau o\upsilon$. See Haenchen, *Acts*, 658, for a slightly different understanding and location of passages which specify Paul's acquittal. He includes an acquittal by Felix (24:23), which is difficult to discern from the text.

39 Acts 26:32. The question frequently raised here is: did the appeal of Paul carry that heavy an imperative? Could not Festus have acquitted Paul then and there regardless of the appeal? Sherwin-White handles the question rather well by stating that this issue 'is not a question of law, but of the relations between the emperor and his subordinates, and of that element of non-constitutional power which the Romans called *auctoritas*, "prestige", on which the supremacy of the Princeps so largely depended. No sensible man with hopes of promotion would dream of short-circuiting the appeal of Caesar unless he had specific authority to do so ... To have acquitted him despite the appeal would have been to offend both the emperor and the province' (*Roman Society*, 65).

40 Dibelius, *Studies*, 213. Haenchen also recognizes that the Lucan political apologetic runs on religious wheels. The Third Evangelist would have his readers see beyond the transparent apology of Paul to discover their own defense to the empire. According to Haenchen, Luke would have his church base its defense, as did the apostle, on the resurrection which ties Christianity to Judaism and renders it a *religio licita* (*Acts*, 99–103, 630–1, 691–4; *ZNTW* LIV [1963] 186). However, continues Haenchen, such a defense would be of little real value, for a Roman judge would not understand an apology based on the resurrection (*Acts*, 101–2, 106–7, 691–4).

We must ask why Luke would expend so much energy promoting a defense which he knew would not be understood by Rome, nor effect a favorable judgment toward the Christian community? Haenchen's exegesis also takes too lightly the serious charges levelled against Paul and the later Christian community (sedition, teaching against established religions), and he does not consider what response Luke may have intended his church to make with respect to these.

41 Luke 9:22; 17:25; 24:7, 26, 44–6; Acts 17:3; 19:21; 23:11; 27:24; see O'Neill, 67–9.

42 Conzelmann, *Theology of St. Luke*, 141–2.

43 *Ibid.*, 144.

44 *Ibid.*

45 H. J. Cadbury, *The Book of Acts in History* (London: A. & C. Black, 1955), touches on the variety of cultural cross-currents – Greek, Roman, Jewish, Oriental – that came in contact with the church of Acts; also see my 'Ignatius of Antioch: The Synthesis of Astral Mysticism, Rational Theology, and Christian Witness,' *Religion in Life* XLVIII (1979).

46 See E. Haenchen, 'The Book of Acts as Source Material for the History of Early Christianity,' *SLA*, 277–8.

47 Acts 28:31.
48 Acts 17:6–9; 18:12–17; 19:28–40 and the last of Paul's trials just described.
49 Acts 16:19–40.
50 Paul's own recollection (2 Cor. 11:25–6) may have provided the nucleus for this construction; see Dibelius, *Studies*, 205–6; Haenchen, *Acts*, 707–10.
51 Williams, *Acts*, 269; F. F. Bruce, *Acts*, 451.
52 Williams, *Acts*, 272; Haenchen, *Acts*, 707.
53 Lake and Cadbury, *BC*, IV, 336.
54 James Smith, *The Voyage and Shipwreck of St Paul* (4th edition, London: Longmans, 1880); Williams, *Acts*, 268–75; Lake and Cadbury, *BC*, IV, 324–5; F. F. Bruce, *Acts*, 451–74.
55 Acts 27:20–36.
56 B. Reicke, 'Die Mahlzeit mit Paulus auf den Wellen des Mittelmeers Act. 27, 33–8,' *ThZ* IV (1948) 401–10, esp. 409.
57 G. H. W. Lampe, 'Acts,' *Peake's Commentary*, 802c; Lake and Cadbury, *BC*, IV, 336.
58 Lake and Cadbury, *ibid.*
59 Lampe, *ibid.*
60 Lampe, *ibid.*
61 Luke 22:17–20. *Didache* IX also has an order different from Matthew, Mark and Paul (1 Cor. 11:23–6; but note the reversed order – wine, bread – in 1 Cor. 10:16). One should also notice that in all of the Acts there is no eucharist as we normally think of it, only the 'breaking of bread' (Acts 2:46).
62 Blass notes the elegant construction of τοῦτο γὰρ πρὸς (with the genitive) τῆς ὑμετέρας σωτηρίας ὑπάρχει; *BD*, 240.
63 I Cor. 11:30.
64 The 'Western' text understood the scene as eucharistic for it adds, ἐπιδιδοὺς καὶ ἡμῖν.
65 Throughout Luke–Acts the 'centurion' has been consistently presented in a highly favorable way. In Luke 7:1–10 Jesus heals the centurion's servant because of the centurion's faith: 'not even in Israel have I found such faith.' A centurion declares Jesus 'truly innocent' at the cross (Luke 23:47). In the book of Acts Cornelius, a 'God-fearer,' becomes the first gentile convert to Christianity (Acts 10), a centurion saves Paul from scourging (Acts 22:25–6), two centurions protect Paul from ambush (Acts 23:23–4), and finally Julius of the Augustan Cohort brings Paul safely to Rome (Acts 27).
66 Haenchen, *Acts*, 708, n. 6; cf. Acts 12:18–19; 16–27.
67 Acts 27:43 (διασῶσαι); also see Luke 7:3 where the centurion asks Jesus to save (διασώσῃ) his servant.
68 Henry Chadwick uses a geometric analogy to describe this shift: from circle (with Jerusalem as the center of the universe) to ellipse (Jerusalem and Rome are the *loci* of authority); 'The Circle and the Ellipse: Rival Concepts of Authority in the Early Church', *Jerusalem and Rome*, 23–36.
69 See above pp. 20–1.

5. Concluding remarks on the political perspective of St Luke

1 *Leg. Gai.* (esp. 67–78, 144–9); *Jos.* 2–3, 38; *Spec.* 4.184–8; *Flac.* 74. Josephus, *JW* 2.390; 3.351–4, 366–96; 5.412.

2 Conzelmann, *Luke*, 16–17, 209–10.
3 Even if one assumes with Robinson a date of AD 60–2 for Luke–Acts, this is also a peaceful time for the church. In his early reign Nero was hailed as a 'Second Augustus,' bringer of the 'golden age' to Rome. Seneca's teaching on mercy (*De Clementia*) seems to have had an effect on the young Nero.
4 S. Benko, 'The History of the Early Roman Empire,' *The Catacombs and the Colosseum*, 62–4; B. Reicke, *The New Testament Era*, tr. by D. E. Green (Philadelphia: Fortress, 1968) 267–71, 291–3. An evaluation of the internal evidence is given by R. Maddox, *The Purpose of Luke–Acts* (Edinburgh: T. & T. Clark, 1982), 80–2; the evidence in Luke–Acts for a church under attack by the state is weak, for 'while Luke acknowledges, along with the other gospel-tradition, that the Christian life is one in which persecution is part of the cost of discipleship, he does not emphasize this more than the other evangelists, and may even be seen to hold out a stronger hope that persecution can be withstood successfully. In Acts this note of confidence in the face of opposition is still stronger' (81). Luke's concern, according to Maddox, was to guard the church from an 'ideology of martyrdom' (96).
5 On the difficulties in positing an anti-Christian persecution under Domitian, see Reicke, *The New Testament Era*, 271–86, 295–301.

In his last few years (93–6) Domitian did reverse the trend toward religious toleration. His attacks, however, were not directed at Judaism or Christianity; rather, he put members of the senatorial class on trial for impiety ($\dot{\alpha}\sigma\dot{\epsilon}\beta\epsilon\iota\alpha$ – disavowal of Roman majesty) and for atheism ($\dot{\alpha}\theta\epsilon\dot{\delta}\tau\eta\varsigma$ – rejection of the state gods). Both charges could be traced to the influence of 'Jewish [or Christian?] inclinations' toward monotheism (Dio Cass., *Hist.* 67.14.2; Suetonius, *Dom.* 12).

We have no solid evidence that even during this period the church could be described as an *ecclesia pressa*. There is nothing in First Clement, including the famous first chapter, that suggests a persecution of the church by Domitian (*contra* Reicke, *The New Testament Era*, 293: '... the First Letter of Clement bears witness to official action against the Christians of Rome.'). There may have been particular Christian believers or sympathizers who were persecuted (e.g. Domitilla and Clemens [?]). Concerning this, Reicke more judiciously concludes that 'Domitian's purpose was domination of the Roman aristocracy, not an attack upon the Christian faith' (302). Cf. T. D. Barnes, 'Legislation against the Christians', *JRS* LVII (1968) 35–6.

Of course the other side of the question is whether the church would have *perceived* Domitian's actions as a threat no matter what he intended. Even if this is answered affirmatively the Christian response seemed to follow one of two paths: to curse the emperor (Rev.) or to pray for him (1 Clem.). Luke certainly would have agreed with the latter approach. See C. Eggenberger, *Die Quellen der Politische Ethik des 1. Klemensbriefes* (Zurich: Zwingli Verlag, 1951).
6 Mark 13; Rev. 13; Sib. 4.117–18; Barn. 2–3.
7 Rom. 13:1–7; also 1 Pet. 2:13–14 and 1 Tim. 2:1–6. For a discussion of these pro-/ and anti-Roman passages see W. L. Knox, 'Church and State in the New Testament,' *JRS* XXXIX (1949) 23–30.
8 1 Thes. 4:13–18; 2 Pet. 3:3–4; 1 Clem. 23.3; 2 Clem. 11.2–3.
9 See E. Earle Ellis, *Eschatology in Luke* (Philadelphia: Fortress, 1972). He

suggests that the problem was not the delay of the parousia, but 'false apocalyptic speculation' (19). Luke was probably dealing with *both* eschatological
problems; see S. G. Wilson, *The Gentiles and the Gentile Mission in Luke–
Acts* (SNTSMS 23; Cambridge: Cambridge University Press, 1973) 83–4.

10 See M. Grant, *The Jews in the Roman World* (New York: Scribner's, 1973)
53–65.

11 Cadbury, *Book of Acts*, 82. More recently, S. G. Wilson has pointed out that
Luke shares this perspective with several contemporary authors; *Luke and the
Pastoral Epistles*, 36–45. One can also find parallels to this not uncommon
theo-political perspective in Plutarch. (*Ad princ. ineru.* 3), Dio Chr. (*Or.* 1.38–
46), Josephus (*JW* 2.390; 5.366–8, 376–8), and Clement of Rome (60.4 –
61.2).

12 C. P. Jones notes that the cynics and apocalyptists fed the uncultured masses a
spicy diet of hatred toward Roman authority, rumors of Roman decadence,
and visions of imminent Roman cataclysm; *Plutarch and Rome* (Oxford: Clarendon Press, 1971) 129.

BIBLIOGRAPHY

1. Primary sources

The Apocrypha and Pseudepigrapha of the Old Testament, 2 vols., ed. by R. H. Charles (Oxford: Clarendon Press, 1913).

The Apocryphal New Testament, 5th impression, tr. by M. R. James (Oxford: Clarendon Press, 1953).

The Apostolic Fathers, 2 vols., with Eng. trans. by K. Lake (LCL; London: Heinemann, 1924–5).

Appian, *Roman History*, 4 vols., with Eng. trans. by H. White (LCL; London: Heinemann, 1912–33).

Biblia Hebraica, ed. by R. Kittel (7th ed.; Stuttgart: Württembergische Bibelanstalt, 1951).

Cicero, *The Verrine Orations*, 2 vols., with Eng. trans. by L. H. G. Greenwood (LCL; London: Heinemann, 1943–53).

The Civil Law, 17 vols., tr. and ed. by S. P. Scott (New York: AMS Press, 1973, orig. publ. 1932).

Corpus Iuris Civilis, 3 vols., ed. by P. Krueger, T. Mommsen and R. Schoell (Berlin: Weidmann, 1872–95).

Dio Cassius, *Roman History*, 9 vols., with Eng. trans. by E. Cary (LCL; London: Heinemann, 1914–27).

Dio Chrysostom, *Orations*, 5 vols. with Eng. trans. by J. W. Cohoon and H. L. Crosby (LCL; London: Heinemann, 1932–51).

Epictetus, *The Discourses as Reported by Arrian, the Manual, and Fragments*, 2 vols., with Eng. trans. by W. A. Oldfather (LCL; London: Heinemann, 1926–8).

Eusebius, *The Ecclesiastical History*, 2 vols., with Eng. trans. by K. Lake (LCL; London: Heinemann, 1926–32).

Fontes iuris romani antejustiniani, 3 vols., ed. by S. Riccobono (Florence: Barbera, 1940–3).

Josephus, *Works*, 9 vols., with Eng. trans. by H. St. J. Thackeray *et al.* (LCL; London: Heinemann, 1926–65).

The Mishnah, tr. by H. Danby (Oxford: Clarendon Press, 1933).

New Testament Apocrypha, 2 vols., ed. by W. Schneemelcher with Eng. trans. by R. McL. Wilson (Philadelphia: Westminster, 1963–5).

Novum Testamentum Graece, ed. by E. Nestle and K. Aland (25th ed., Stuttgart: Württembergische Bibelanstalt, 1975).

Philo, *Works*, 10 vols., with Eng. trans. by F. H. Colson, G. H. Whitaker, and R. Marcus (LCL; London: Heinemann, 1929–53).

Pliny (the younger), *Letters and Panegyricus*, 2 vols., with Eng. trans.
  by B. Radice (LCL; London: Heinemann, 1969).
Pliny, *Natural History*, 10 vols., with Eng. trans. by H. Rackham (LCL;
  London: Heinemann, 1938–63).
Plutarch, *Moralia*, 10 vols. with Eng. trans. by F. C. Babbitt *et al.* (LCL;
  London: Heinemann, 1927–69).
  The Parallel Lives, 10 vols., with Eng. trans. by B. Perrin (LCL;
  London: Heinemann, 1914–26).
Seneca, *Epistulae Morales*, 3 vols., with Eng. trans. by R. M. Gummere
  (LCL; London: Heinemann, 1917–25).
Septuaginta, 2 vols., ed. by A. Rahlfs (6th ed., Stuttgart: Württem ber-
  gische Bibelanstalt, 1952).
Strabo, *Geography*, 8 vols., with Eng. trans. by H. L. Jones (LCL; London:
  Heinemann, 1917–32).
Suetonius, *The Lives of the Caesars and the Lives of Illustrious Men*,
  2 vols. with Eng. trans. by J. C. Rolfe (LCL; London: Heinemann,
  1914).
Tacitus, *The Annals*, 3 vols., with Eng. trans. by J. Jackson (LCL; London:
  Heinemann, 1931–7).
  The Histories, 2 vols., with Eng. trans. by C. H. Moore (LCL; London:
  Heinemann, 1925–31).
Velleius Paterculus and Res Gestae Divi Augusti, with Eng. trans. by F. W.
  Shipley (LCL; London: Heinemann, 1961).
Virgil, *Aeneid and Minor Poems*, 2 vols., with Eng. trans. by H. R. Fair-
  clough (LCL; London: Heinemann, 1927).
  Bucolica et Georgica, with introduction and notes by T. E. Page (Lon-
  don: Macmillan, 1963).

2. Books, commentaries, and other reference works

Aune, D. E., ed., *Studies in the New Testament and Early Christian
  Literature* (Leiden: Brill, 1972).
Bailey, C., ed., *The Legacy of Rome* (Oxford: Clarendon Press, 1924).
Barrett, C. K., *Luke the Historian in Recent Study* (Philadelphia: Fortress,
  1970).
  New Testament Essays (London: SPCK, 1972).
  The Second Epistle to the Corinthians (HNTC; New York: Harper,
  1973).
Bauer, B., *Die Apostelgeschichte, eine Ausgleichung des Paulinismus und
  des Judenthums innerhalb der christlichen Kirche* (Berlin: G. Hempel,
  1850).
Bauer, W., *A Greek–English Lexicon of the New Testament and Other
  Early Christian Literature*, tr. and adapted by W. F. Arndt and F.
  W. Gingrich (Chicago: University of Chicago Press, 1957).
Baur, F. C., *Paulus, der Apostel Jesu Christi*, I Teil (Leipzig: Fues, 1866).

Beare, F. W., *The Epistle to the Philippians* (HNTC; New York: Harper, 1959).

Benko, S. and J. O'Rourke, eds., *The Catacombs and the Colosseum* (Valley Forge, PA: Judson Press, 1971).

Betz, H. D., ed., *Plutarch's Ethical Writings and Early Christian Literature* (Leiden: Brill, 1978).

Black, M. and H. H. Rowley, *Peake's Commentary on the Bible* (London: Nelson, 1962).

Blass, F. and A. DeBrunner, *A Greek Grammar of the New Testament and Other Early Christian Literature*, tr. by R. Funk (Chicago: University of Chicago Press, 1961).

Blinzler, J., *The Trial of Jesus*, tr. by I. and F. McHugh (Westminster, MD: Newman, 1959).

Brandon, S. G. F., *The Fall of Jerusalem and the Christian Church* (London: SPCK, 1951).

   Jesus and the Zealots (New York: Scribner's, 1967).

   The Trial of Jesus of Nazareth (New York: Stein & Day, 1968).

Brown, R., *The Birth of the Messiah* (Garden City, NY: Doubleday, 1977).

Bruce, F. F., *The Acts of the Apostles* (London: Tyndale, 1951).

Bultmann, R., *History of the Synoptic Tradition*, tr. by J. Marsh (New York: Harper & Row, 1968).

   Theology of the New Testament, 2 vols., tr. by K. Grobel, (New York: Scribner's, 1955).

Burnside, W. F., *The Acts of the Apostles* (Cambridge: Cambridge University Press, 1916).

   The Gospel According to St. Luke (Cambridge: Cambridge University Press, 1913).

Cadbury, H. J., *The Making of Luke–Acts* (London: SPCK, 1927; reprinted 1968).

   The Style and Literary Method of Luke (Cambridge, MA: Harvard University, 1920).

   The Book of Acts in History (London: A. & C. Black, 1955).

Cadoux, C. J., *The Early Church and the World* (Edinburgh: Clark, 1925).

Caird, G. B., *The Gospel of St. Luke* (Baltimore: Penguin, 1964).

Cassidy, R., *Jesus, Politics, and Society* (Maryknoll, NY: Orbis, 1978).

Cochrane, C. N., *Christianity and Classical Culture* (New York: Galaxy, 1957).

Conzelmann, H., *Die Apostelgeschichte* (HNT; Tübingen: Mohr, 1963).

   Die Mitte der Zeit (Tübingen: Mohr, 1953).

   The Theology of St. Luke, trans. of *Die Mitte der Zeit* by Geoffrey Buswell (New York: Harper and Row, 1960).

Cramer, F. J., *Astrology in Roman Law and Politics* (Philadelphia: American Philosophical Society, 1954).

Creed, J. M., *The Gospel According to St. Luke* (London: Macmillan, 1930).

Cullmann, O., *The Christology of the New Testament*, tr. by S. C. Guthrie and C. A. M. Hall (London: SCM, 1959).

   Peter: Disciple, Apostle, Martyr, tr. by F. Filson (rev. edition, Philadelphia: Westminster, 1962).

The State in the New Testament (New York: Scribner's, 1956).
Danker, F. W., *Jesus and the New Age* (St Louis: Clayton Publishing House, 1972).
Luke (Philadelphia: Fortress, 1976).
Deissmann, A., *Light from the Ancient East*, tr. by L. Strachan (London: Doran, 1927).
Dibelius, M., *An die Thessalonicher I, II, An die Philipper* (HNT; Tübingen: Mohr, 1937).
Botschaft und Geschichte, 2 vols. (Tübingen: Mohr, 1953–56).
From Tradition to Gospel, tr. by B. L. Woolf (New York: Scribner's, 1935).
Studies in the Acts of the Apostles, tr. by Mary Ling and Paul Schubert (New York: Scribner's, 1956).
Dodd, C. H., *The Apostolic Preaching and Its Developments* (London: Hodder and Stoughton, 1936).
More New Testament Studies (Grand Rapids, MI: Eerdmans, 1968).
New Testament Studies (New York: Scribner's, 1954).
Duncan, G. S., *St. Paul's Ephesian Ministry* (New York: Scribner's, 1930).
Easton, B. S., *Early Christianity* (Greenwich, CT: Seabury, 1954).
The Gospel According to St. Luke (New York: Scribner's, 1926).
Eggenberger, C., *Die Quellen der politische Ethik des 1. Klemensbriefes* (Zurich: Zwingli Verlag, 1951).
Ehrhardt, A., *The Acts of the Apostles* (Manchester: Manchester University Press, 1969).
Eisler, R., *The Messiah Jesus and John the Baptist*, tr. by A. H. Krappe (New York: Dial Press, 1931).
Elliott, J. K., ed., *Studies in New Testament Language and Text* (Leiden: Brill, 1976).
Ellis, E. E., *Eschatology in Luke* (Philadelphia: Fortress, 1972).
The Gospel of Luke (rev. edition, London: Marshall, Morgan and Scott, 1974).
Ferguson, J., *The Religions of the Roman Empire* (Ithaca, NY: Cornell University, 1970).
Fitzmyer, J., *The Gospel According to Luke*, to be 2 vols., only Vol. I published (AB; Garden City, NY: Doubleday, 1981).
Flender, H., *St. Luke: Theologian of Redemptive History*, tr. by Reginald and Ilse Fuller (Philadelphia: Fortress, 1967).
Foakes Jackson, F. J., and K. Lake, *The Beginnings of Christianity*, 5 vols. (London: Macmillan, 1920–33).
Fowler, W. W., *The Religious Experience of the Roman People* (London: Macmillan, 1911).
Frank, T., ed., *An Economic Survey of Ancient Rome*, 6 vols., (Baltimore: Johns Hopkins University Press, 1933–41).
Franklin, E., *Christ the Lord: A Study in the Purpose and Theology of Luke–Acts* (Philadelphia: Westminster, 1975).
Frend, W. H. C., *Martyrdom and Persecution in the Early Church* (Oxford: Blackwell, 1965).
Gärtner, B., *The Areopagus Speech and Natural Revelation*, tr. by C. H. King (ASNU 21; Uppsala: C. W. K. Gleerup, 1955).

The Temple and the Community in Qumran and the New Testament (SNTSMS 1; Cambridge: Cambridge University Press, 1965).

Gasque, W., *A History of the Criticism of the Acts of the Apostles* (Tübingen: Mohr, 1975).

Gasque, W., and R. P. Martin, eds., *Apostolic History and the Gospel* (Grand Rapids, MI: Eerdmans, 1970).

Gaston, L., *No Stone on Another* (Leiden: Brill, 1970).

Gnilka, J., *Die Philipperbrief* (HThKNT; Freiburg: Herder, 1968).

Godet, F., *Commentary on the Gospel of St Luke*, 2 vols., Vol. I tr. by E. W. Shalders and Vol. II tr. by M. D. Cusin (Edinburgh: T. & T. Clark, 1870).

Goodenough, E. R., *The Politics of Philo Judaeus* (New Haven, CT: Yale University, 1938).

Goodspeed, E. J., *Introduction to the New Testament* (Chicago: University of Chicago Press, 1937).

Grant, F. C., *The Gospels: Their Origin and Growth* (New York: Harper, 1957).

Grant, M., *The Jews in the Roman World* (New York: Scribner's, 1973).

Grant, R. M., ed., *The Apostolic Fathers*, 6 vols. (New York: Nelson, 1964).

Grenier, A., *The Roman Spirit in Religion, Thought, and Art* (New York: Cooper Square Publishers, 1926, reprinted 1970).

Grundmann, W., *Das Evangelium nach Lukas* (THNT; Berlin: Evangelische Verlagsanstalt, 1971).

Haenchen, E., *The Acts of the Apostles*, tr. from 14th edition by Bernard Noble and Gerald Shinn, with the translation revised by R. McL. Wilson (Philadelphia: Westminster, 1971).

Die Apostelgeschichte (KEK; 14th ed., Göttingen: Vandenhoeck und Ruprecht 1965).

Hanson, R. P. C., *The Acts* (Oxford: Clarendon Press, 1967).

Harnack, *The Acts of the Apostles*, tr. by J. R. Wilkinson, (London: Williams & Norgate, 1909).

The Date of the Acts and the Synoptic Gospels, tr. by J. R. Wilkinson (London: Williams & Norgate, 1911).

Luke the Physician, tr. by J. R. Wilkinson (London: Williams & Norgate, 1907).

The Mission and Expansion of Christianity, 2 vols., tr. by J. Moffatt (rev. edition, New York: G. P. Putnam, 1908).

Hengel, M., *Die Zeloten* (Leiden: Brill, 1961).

Herford, R. T., *Christianity in Talmud and Midrash* (Clifton, NJ: Reference Book Publishers, 1903, reprinted 1966).

Hoehner, H. W., *Herod Antipas* (SNTSMS 17; Cambridge; Cambridge University Press, 1972).

Hughes, P. E., *Paul's Second Epistle to the Corinthians* (Grand Rapids, MI: Eerdmans, 1962).

Jeremias, J., *Jerusalem in the Time of Jesus*, tr. by F. H. and C. H. Cave (Philadelphia, PA: Fortress, 1969).

Jervell, J., *Luke and the People of God* (Minneapolis, MN: Augsburg, 1972).

Johnson, S., ed., *The Joy of Study* (New York: Macmillan, 1951).
Jones, A. H. M., *A History of Rome Through the Fifth Century*, 2 vols. (New York: Walker, 1968–70).
The Later Roman Empire, 2 vols., (Oxford: Blackwell, 1964).
Studies in Roman Government and Law (New York: Praeger, 1960).
The Herods of Judaea (Oxford: Clarendon Press, 1938).
Jones, C. P., *Plutarch and Rome* (Oxford: Clarendon Press, 1971).
Juel, D., *An Introduction to New Testament Literature* (Nashville, TN: Abingdon, 1978).
Keck, L., and J. L. Martyn, eds., *Studies in Luke–Acts* (Nashville, TN: Abingdon, 1966).
Kennard, J. S., *Render to God: A Study of the Tribute Passage* (Oxford: Oxford University Press, 1950).
Kittel, G., and others, *Theological Dictionary of the New Testament*, 10 vols., tr. and ed. by G. W. Bromiley (Grand Rapids, MI: Eerdmans, 1964–76).
Klostermann, E., *Das Lukasevangelium* (HNT; Tübingen: Mohr, 1929).
Knox, W. L., *Some Hellenistic Elements in Primitive Christianity* (London: H. Milford, 1944).
The Sources of the Synoptic Gospels, 2 vols., ed. by H. Chadwick (Cambridge: Cambridge University Press, 1953).
Kümmel, W. G., P. Feine and J. Behm, *Introduction to the New Testament*, tr. by A. J. Mattill (Nashville, TN: Abingdon, 1966).
Lewis, N. and M. Reinhold, *Roman Civilization*, 2 vols. (New York: Columbia University, 1951, 1955).
Löning, K., *Die Saulustradition in der Apostelgeschichte* (Münster: Verlag Aschendorff, 1973).
Lohmeyer, E., *Der Brief an die Philipper* (KEK; Göttingen: Vandenhoeck & Ruprecht, 1929, reprinted 1974).
Luce, H. K., *The Gospel According to St Luke* (Cambridge: Cambridge University Press, 1936).
Maddox, R., *The Purpose of Luke–Acts* (Edinburgh: T. & T. Clark, 1982).
Manson, T. W., *The Sayings of Jesus as Recorded in the Gospels of St Matthew and St Luke* (London: SCM, 1954).
Manson, W., *The Gospel of Luke* (MNTC; New York: R. R. Smith, 1930).
Marshall, I. H., *The Gospel of Luke* (Exeter: Paternoster, 1978).
Luke: Historian and Theologian (Grand Rapids, MI: Zondervan, 1971).
Martin, R. P., *Philippians* (NCB; London: Oliphants, 1976).
Marxsen, W., *Introduction to the New Testament*, tr. by G. Buswell (Philadelphia, PA: Fortress, 1968).
Mark the Evangelist (Nashville, TN: Abingdon, 1969).
Michael, J. H., *The Epistle of Paul to the Philippians* (MNTC; New York: Harper, 1928).
Michaelis, W., *Die Datierung des Philipperbriefs* (Gütersloh: Bertelsmann, 1933).
Mommsen, T., *Römisches Strafrecht* (Leipzig: Duncker & Humbolt, 1899).
Moore, G. F., *Judaism in the First Centuries of the Christian Era*, 3 vols. (Cambridge, MA: Harvard University, 1927–30).
Morrison, C. D., *The Powers That Be* (SBT 29; Naperville, IL: Allenson, 1960).

Moule, C. F. D., *An Idiom Book of New Testament Greek* (2nd edition, Cambridge: Cambridge University Press, 1959).

Munck, J., *The Acts of the Apostles* (AB 31; Garden City: Doubleday, 1967).

Nilsson, M. P., *Imperial Rome* (New York: Schocken, 1962).

Nock, A. D., *Essays on Religion and the Ancient World*, 2 vols., ed. by Z. Stewart (Oxford: Clarendon Press, 1972).

Ogg, G., *The Chronology of Paul* (London: Epworth Press, 1968).

O'Neill, J. C., *The Theology of Acts in Its Historical Setting* (London: SPCK, 1979).

Parker, H. M. D., *The Roman Legions* (Oxford: Clarendon Press, 1928).

Plummer, A., *The Gospel According to St. Luke* (ICC; Edinburgh: T. & T. Clark, 1896).

Quasten, J., *Patrology*, 3 vols. (Utrecht–Antwerp: Spectrum, 1950–60).

Radl, W., *Paulus und Jesus im lukanischen Doppelwerk* (Frankfort: H. Lang, 1975).

Ramsay, W. M., *St Paul the Traveller and the Roman Citizen* (New York: Putnam, 1896).

Was Christ Born at Bethlehem? (New York: Putnam, 1898).

Reicke, B., *The New Testament Era*, tr. by D. E. Green (Philadelphia: Fortress, 1968).

Robinson, J. A. T., *Redating the New Testament* (Philadelphia, PA: Westminster, 1976).

Robinson, W. C., Jr, *The Way of the Lord* (Basel: Universitätsverlag, 1960).

Rogers, R. S., *Criminal Trials and Criminal Legislation under Tiberius* (Middletown, CT: American Philological Association, 1935).

Sahlin, H., *Der Messias und das Gottesvolk* (ASNU 12; Uppsala: Almqvist and Wiksells, 1945).

Sanders, E. P., *Paul and Rabbinic Judaism* (Philadelphia, PA: Fortress, 1977).

Schmidt, K. L., *Der Rahmen der Geschichte Jesu* (Berlin: Trowitzsch & Sohn, 1919).

Schmithals, W., *Das Evangelium nach Lukas* (Zurich: Theologischer Verlag, 1980).

Paul and the Gnostics, tr. by J. E. Steely (Nashville, TN: Abingdon, 1972).

Schneckenburger, M., *Über den Zweck der Apostelgeschichte* (Bern: Christian Fischer, 1841).

Schrader, K., *Der Apostel Paulus*, 5 vols. (Leipzig: Christian Ernst Hollmann, 1836).

Schürer, E., *A History of the Jewish People in the Age of Jesus Christ*, 2 vols. (Edinburgh: T. & T. Clark, rev. edition, 1973).

Schwegler, A., *Das Nachapostolische Zeitalter in den Hauptmomenten seiner Entwicklung*, 2 vols. (Tübingen: Fucs, 1846).

Sevenster, J. N., *Paul and Seneca* (Leiden: Brill, 1961).

Sherwin-White, A. N., *Roman Society and Roman Law in the New Testament* (Oxford: Oxford University Press, 1963).

Smith, J., *The Voyage and Shipwreck of St. Paul*, 4th edition, (London: Longmans, 1880).

Stauffer, E., *Christ and the Caesars*, tr. by K. and R. G. Smith (Philadelphia, PA: Westminster, 1952).
Streeter, B. H., *The Four Gospels* (rev. edition, New York: Macmillan, 1930).
Talbert, C., *Literary Patterns, Theological Themes and the Genre of Luke–Acts* (SBLMS 20; Missoula: Scholars Press, 1974).
Luke and the Gnostics (Nashville, TN: Abingdon, 1966).
Perspectives on Luke–Acts (Dansville, VA: Association of Baptist Professors of Religion, 1978).
Taylor, L. R., *The Divinity of the Roman Emperor* (Middletown, CT: American Philological Association, 1931, reprinted 1975).
Taylor, V., *Behind the Third Gospel: A Study of the Proto-Luke Hypothesis* (Oxford: Clarendon Press, 1926).
The Passion Narrative of St Luke, ed. by O. E. Evans (SNTSMS 19; Cambridge: Cambridge University Press, 1972).
Thompson, G. H. P., *The Gospel According to Luke* (Oxford: Oxford University Press, 1972).
Vincent, M. R., *A Critical and Exegetical Commentary on the Epistles to the Philippians and to Philemon* (ICC; Edinburgh: T. & T. Clark, 1897, reprinted 1961).
Webster, G., *The Roman Imperial Army of the First and Second Centuries AD* (New York: Funk & Wagnalls, 1969).
Weiss, J., *Über die Absicht und den literarischen Charakter der Apostel-Geschichte* (Marburg: Vandenhoeck & Ruprecht, 1897).
Williams, C. S. C., *The Acts of the Apostles* (HNTC; New York: Harper, 1957).
Wilson, S. G., *The Gentiles and the Gentile Mission in Luke–Acts* (SNTSMS 23; Cambridge: Cambridge University Press, 1973).
Luke and the Pastoral Epistles (London: SPCK, 1979).
Winter, P., *On the Trial of Jesus* (Berlin: De Gruyter, 1961).
Zeller, E., *The Contents and Origin of the Acts of the Apostles*, 2 vols., tr. by J. Dare (London: Williams & Norgate, 1875).

3. Periodical Articles

Barnes, T. D., 'Legislation against the Christians,' *JRS* LVII (1968).
Barnett, P. W., '*Apographe* and *apographesthai* in Luke 2:1–5,' *ExpT* LXXXV (1973–4).
Barrett, C. K., 'Pauline Controversies in the Post-Pauline Period,' *NTS* XX (1973–4).
Baur, F. C., 'Über den Ursprung des Episcopats,' *TZT* 1938, Heft 3.
'Über Zweck und Veranlassung des Römerbriefs und die damit zusammenhängenden Verhältnisse der römischen Gemeinde,' *TZT* 1836, Heft 3.
Braunert, H., 'Der römische Provinzialzensus und der Schätzungsbericht des Lukas-Evangeliums,' *Historia* VI (1957).
Cadbury, H. J., 'The Purpose Expressed in Luke's Preface,' *The Expositor* XXI, 126 (1921).
Charlesworth, M. P., 'Some Observations on the Ruler-Cult, Especially in Rome,' *HTR* XXVIII (1935).

Chilton, C. W., 'The Roman Law of Treason under the Early Principate,' *JRS* LXV (1965).

Conzelmann, H., 'Geschichte, Geschichtsbild und Geschichtsdarstellung bei Lukas,' *TLZ* LXXXV (1960).

Dibelius, M., 'Herodes und Pilatus,' *ZNTW* XVI (1915).

Enslin, M., '"Luke" and Paul,' *JAOS* LVIII (1938).
'Once Again, Luke and Paul,' *ZNTW* LXI (1970).

Garnsey, P., 'The *Lex Iulia* and Appeal under the Empire,' *JRS* LVIII (1966).

Gasque, W., 'The Historical Value of the Book of Acts,' *The Evangelical Quarterly* XLI (1969).

Goodman, F. W., 'Sources of the First Two Chapters in Matthew and Luke,' *CQR* 162 (1961).

Haenchen, E., 'Judentum und Christentum in der Apostelgeschichte,' *ZNTW* LIV (1963).

Harrison, P. N., 'The Pastoral Epistles and Duncan's Ephesian Theory,' *NTS* II (1965–6).

Jewett, R., 'The Epistolary Thanksgiving and the Integrity of Philippians,' *NovT* XII (1970).

Karris, R., 'Missionary Communities: A New Paradigm for the Study of Luke–Acts,' *CBQ* XLI (1, 1979).

Kilpatrick, G. D., 'A Theme of the Lucan Passion Story and Luke xxiii, 47,' *JTS* XLIII (1942).

Knox, W. L., 'Church and State in the New Testament,' *JRS* XXXIX (1949).

Miles, G., and G. Trompf, 'Luke and Antiphon: The Theology of Acts 27–8 in the Light of Pagan Beliefs about Divine Retribution, Pollution, and Shipwreck,' *HTR* LXIX (1967).

Neyrey, J. H., 'Jesus' Address to the Women of Jerusalem (Lk. 23:27–31) – A Prophetic Judgement Oracle,' *NTS* XXIX (1983).

Ogg, G., 'The Quirinius Question Today,' *ExpT* LXXIX (1968).

Oliver, H. H., 'The Lukan Birth Stories and the Purpose of Luke–Acts,' *NTS* X (1964).

Pesch, R., 'Die Vision des Stephanus Apg. 7, 55ff., im Rahmen der Apostelgeschichte,' *Bib. Leben* IX (1965).

Pfister, F., 'Die zweimalige römische Gefangenschaft und die spanische Reise des Apostels Paulus und der Schluss der Apostelgeschichte,' *ZNTW* XIV (1913).

Pollard, T. E., 'The Integrity of Philippians,' *NTS* XIII (1966–7).

Ramsay, W. M., 'The Imprisonment and Supposed Trial of St. Paul in Rome,' *Expositor* 8/V (1913).
'Luke's Narrative of the Birth of Jesus,' *Expositor* 8/IV (1912).

Reicke, B., 'Die Mahlzeit mit Paulus auf den Wellen des Mittelmeers Act. 27, 33–38,' *ThZ* (1948).

Rogers, R. S., 'Treason in the Early Empire,' *JRS* LXIX (1959).

Sneen, D. J., 'An Exegesis of Luke 1:1–4 with Special Regard to Luke's Purpose as Historian,' *ExpT* LXXXIII (1971).

Talbert, C., 'Shifting Sands: The Recent Study of the Gospel of Luke,' *Interpretation* XXX (1976).

Tyson, J. B., 'The Opposition to Jesus in the Gospel of Luke,' *Pers Rel Stud* V (1978).
Walaskay, P. W., 'Ignatius of Antioch: The Synthesis of Astral Mysticism, Rational Theology, and Christian Witness,' *Religion in Life* XLVIII (1979).
Ziesler, J. A., 'Luke and the Pharisees,' *NTS* XXV (1979).

4. Essays

Barrett, C. K., 'The Acts – of Paul,' *New Testament Essays* (London: SPCK, 1972).
    'The New Testament Doctrine of Church and State,' *New Testament Essays* (London: SPCK, 1972).
Benko, S., 'The History of the Early Roman Empire,' *The Catacombs and the Colosseum* (Valley Forge, PA: Judson Press, 1971).
Brown, R. E., 'Luke's Method in the Annunciation Narrative of Chapter One,' *PLA*.
Brown, S., 'The Role of the Prologues in Determining the Purpose of Luke–Acts,' *PLA*.
Cadbury, H. J., 'Commentary on the Preface of Luke,' *BC*, II, App. C.
    'Roman Law and the Trial of Paul,' *BC* V.
Chadwick, H., 'The Circle and the Ellipse: Rival Concepts of Authority in The Early Church,' *Jerusalem and Rome* (Philadelphia, PA: Fortress, 1966).
Clark, K. W., 'The Meaning of [Kata] kyrieuein,' *Studies in New Testament Language and Text*, ed. by J. K. Elliott (Leiden: Brill, 1976).
Conzelmann, H., 'Luke's Place in the Development of Early Christianity,' *SLA*.
Cook, F. C., 'The Acts of the Apostles,' *The Bible Commentary* (New York: Scribner's, 1895).
Deissmann, A., 'Zur ephesinischen Gefangenschaft des Apostels Paulus,' *Anatolian Studies Presented to Sir W. M. Ramsay*, ed. by W. H. Buckler and W. M. Calder (Manchester: Manchester University Press, 1923).
Dodd, C. H., 'The Mind of Paul,' *New Testament Studies* (New York: Scribner's, 1953).
    'The Fall of Jerusalem and the "Abomination of Desolation",' *More New Testament Studies* (Grand Rapids, MI: Eerdmans, 1968).
Easton, B. S., 'The Purpose of Acts,' *Early Christianity* (Greenwich, CT: Seabury, 1954).
Filson, D., 'The Journey Motif in Luke–Acts,' *Apostolic History and the Gospel*, ed. by W. Gasque and R. P. Martin (Grand Rapids, MI: Eerdmans, 1970).
Findlay, J. A., 'Luke,' *Abingdon Bible Commentary* (New York: Abingdon, 1929).
Foakes Jackson, F. J. and K. Lake, 'The Zealots', *BC*, I, App. A.
Haenchen, E., 'The Book of Acts as Source Material for Early Christianity,' *SLA*.

Heichelheim, F. M., 'Roman Syria,' *An Economic Survey of Ancient Rome*, IV, ed. by Tenney Frank (Baltimore: Johns Hopkins University, 1938).

Jones, A. H. M., 'I Appeal unto Caesar,' *Studies in Roman Government and Law* (New York: Praeger, 1960).

'Imperial and Senatorial Jurisdiction in the Early Principate,' *Studies in Roman Government and Law*.

Jones, H. S., 'Administration,' *The Legacy of Rome*, ed. by C. Bailey (Oxford: Clarendon Press, 1923).

Knowling, R. J., 'The Acts of the Apostles,' *The Expositor's Greek Testament*, II, ed. by W. R. Nicoll (New York: Dodd, Mead, & Co., 1900).

Knox, J., 'Acts and the Pauline Letter Corpus,' *SLA*.

Lake, K., 'Proselytes and God-fearers,' *BC* V.

'What was the End of St. Paul's Trial?' quoted in *BC* V, 326–32.

Lampe, G. W. H., 'Luke,' *PCB* (London: Nelson, 1962).

'Acts,' *PCB*.

Mattill, A. J., 'The Purpose of Acts: Schneckenburger Reconsidered,' *Apostolic History and the Gospel*, ed. by W. Gasque and R. Martin (Grand Rapids, MI: Eerdmans, 1970).

'The Value of Acts as a Source for the Study of Paul,' *PLA*.

McGiffert, A. C., 'The Historical Criticism of Acts in Germany,' *BC* II.

Minear, P., 'Luke's Use of the Birth Stories,' *SLA*.

Moehring, H., 'The Census in Luke as an Apologetic Device,' *Studies in the New Testament and Early Christian Literature*, ed. by D. E. Aune (Leiden: Brill, 1972).

Nock, A. D., 'The Augustan Restoration,' *Essays on Religion in The Ancient World*, I, ed. by Z. Stewart (Oxford: Clarendon Press, 1972).

'The Emperor's Divine *Comes*,' *Essays on Religion in the Ancient World*, II.

'Religious Developments from the Close of the Republic to the Death of Nero,' *CAH*, X.

'Soter and Euergetes,' *The Joy of Study*, ed. by Sherman E. Johnson (New York: Macmillan, 1951).

Quinn, J. D., 'The Last Volume of Luke: the Relation of Luke–Acts to the Pastoral Epistles,' *PLA*.

Reicke, B., 'Caesarea, Rome, and the Captivity Epistles,' *Apostolic History and the Gospel*, ed. by W. Gasque and R. P. Martin (Grand Rapids, MI: Eerdmans, 1970).

'Synoptic Prophecies on the Destruction of Jerusalem,' *Studies in the New Testament and Early Christian Literature*, ed. by D. E. Aune (Leiden: Brill, 1972).

Robbins, V., 'Prefaces in Greco-Roman Biography and Luke–Acts,' *SBL 1978 Seminar Papers*, II (Missoula, MT: Scholars Press, 1978).

Stevenson, G. H., 'The Imperial Administration,' *CAH*, X.

Unnik, W. C. van, 'Luke–Acts, A Storm Center in Contemporary Scholarship,' *SLA*.

Vielhauer, P., 'On the Paulinism of Acts,' *SLA*.

INDEX OF PASSAGES CITED

115